RELIGION AND SOCIAL WORK

RELIGION AND CIVILIZATION SERIES

RELIGION AND SOCIAL WORK

EDITED BY

F. Ernest Johnson

PROFESSOR EMERITUS OF EDUCATION, TEACHERS
COLLEGE, COLUMBIA UNIVERSITY

Published by

The INSTITUTE for RELIGIOUS and SOCIAL STUDIES *, Jewish*

Distributed by

HARPER & BROTHERS *Theological Seminary of America*

NEW YORK

PRINTED IN THE UNITED STATES OF AMERICA
BY THE VAIL-BALLOU PRESS, INC., BINGHAMTON, N.Y.

This volume is based on lectures given at The Institute for Religious and Social Studies of The Jewish Theological Seminary of America during the winter of 1953–1954. Chaplain Otis R. Rice, Executive Director, Department of Pastoral Services, The National Council of Churches of Christ in the United States of America, gave an address on "The Institutional Chaplaincy," but unfortunately was prevented from preparing the material for publication.

Each chapter in this volume represents solely the individual opinion of the author. Neither the Institute nor the editor assumes responsibility for the views expressed. The contributors were invited to address the Institute because of the special contribution each could make to general knowledge of the subject.

This is a Jacob Ziskind Memorial publication.

FOREWORD

This series of addresses has a double purpose: to afford a perspective on the social welfare activities of American churches and synagogues, and to point up issues of theology and social policy that are giving concern both to the ministry and to lay leaders in relation to the social outreach of religion. The participants, who write authoritatively and out of experience, were for the most part assigned separate topics, but with full realization that there would be a considerable "overlap." This was all to the good, since it resulted in a symposium of views on certain fundamental questions.

Chapter XI records a panel discussion by several persons focused on the church-state issue. It seemed desirable to attack this highly controversial phase of our subject by presenting an agreed syllabus of questions to a selected group of informed and experienced persons.

For a variety of reasons, preparation of the addresses for publication has been delayed. Because of this the text has been modified here and there to take account of developments that have taken place since the series was delivered.

The editor has attempted in the final chapter to draw together the threads of the entire discussion and to locate points that warrant emphasis. He hopes this has been done with a minimum of individual bias.

It will be at once apparent that each writer was free to discuss the topic assigned without any stipulation as to uniformity in organization. In editing the addresses for publication care has been taken not to do violence to individual style, nor to curtail the freedom of a writer to elaborate his or her subject beyond the limits of the oral presentation.

If the reader is troubled by the inconclusiveness of the handling of philosophical and doctrinal issues that here and there emerge, he may be interested to learn that the next volume in this series will be on the subject, "Contemporary Patterns of Faith."

THE EDITOR

April 23, 1956

CONTENTS

I

THE CHURCH AND HUMAN WELFARE

BY

ARTHUR L. SWIFT, JR.

*Professor of Church and Community,
Union Theological Seminary*

It is my task, I think, to set the stage and speak the prologue for the distinguished performers to follow. In somewhat sketchy fashion, as on Shakespeare's stage signs read: "This is a castle," "Here is a wood," I will try to indicate some of the historical facts that give meaning to the action and to offer what seems to me a proper interpretation of the task of church and of welfare in our social life today. As later the actors appear one after another and the play unfolds, you will judge my frank opinions and correct them where they are wrong.

At the outset I want to get this straight: human welfare is not the *primary* concern of the Church. Its central purpose is to "glorify God and enjoy Him forever," through worship to build and to sustain the means whereby man and God may become more closely related. Concern for the humanity of man to man results inevitably from this communion with a God of love and justice, but is always secondary to it and dependent upon it in so far as it is in any sense religious.

But this, too, must be realized: the Church has a unique and distinctive concern for human welfare as being the desire and will of God and therefore in a particular sense sustained within the structure of His Creation. Efforts to improve the lot of men and women and children are in the direction and movement of God's

I

love in a universe where at long last love must prove stronger than hate. This conviction goes far to explain the vast involvement of organized religion in the business of human welfare. But the degree of effort any religious group expends upon human welfare is in large measure influenced by its theology, especially its doctrines of man and of salvation. Another major factor is the extent to which other agencies of human welfare have preempted the field. In spite of recent reverses at the hands of Republicanism, the welfare state towers over all competitors. To these complex and troublesome issues I shall return in my effort to sketch in outline a theory of relationship between the Church and human welfare. But first let me suggest the historical facts that help to explain the theory.

Synagogue and Church are the progenitors of charity. Out of ancient Israel's concern for justice and mercy toward the sick, the poor, the motherless, the widowed, from Micah and Hosea, Jeremiah and Isaiah, grew the compassion of Jesus, the devotion of Paul. The justice and love of God thus set forth and exemplified in the Judeo-Christian tradition have given drive and direction to man's charities. Historically the whole shape and operation of organized welfare is inexplicable apart from the religious conviction and commitment at the vital heart of our sacred Scriptures. Without laboring the obvious, let us glance back toward the beginnings of man's social concerns, if only briefly, so as to gain perspective upon the two major issues we must face, the relation of man to God and to government in his efforts toward human welfare.

Human welfare, an active concern for the well-being of others within the social group, had its beginnings before man became fully man. Its essence is found in the nurture of offspring, the mother's care for her child. Religion, too, has been traced into prehistory, its symbols found in Cro-Magnon cave paintings and in ancient burial mounds. Religion in its simplest expression is a belief in spiritual power or powers, usually personal, and an effort to establish rewarding relations with them. Social welfare grew out of parental love to include, by unconscious imitation, a similar affection between brothers and sisters. Then, less intensively, it took in the clan, and even the visiting stranger. As civilization developed, so did the ways in which a fellow could get into trouble; the more advanced the civilization, the larger the number of ways, and the more prevalent the agencies, public, private, and commercial, to deal with them. Social welfare has now become a profession.

Religion has had a somewhat different development. It was professionalized much, much earlier; and earlier became a vested interest. But, almost at the start, religion and social welfare got together. The gods of the tribe were believed to take an interest in the tribe's well-being. At all events the chiefs and rulers learned that these gods, or ghosts, or demons, once committed to a thing, saw to it that the tribesmen did not forget it. And so religion worked to reinforce the social welfare of the group. It was used by the powerful in the group to give divine sanction to those ways of behaving that to them seemed salutary.

The very title of this paper tends to place religion and welfare over against one another. But we know that they have been together a long, long while. Indeed, the primitive civilizations, while they distinguished between the sacred and the secular, kept them pretty closely interrelated. If the Trobriand Islanders planted yams or the North American Plains Indians planted corn, the ground had to be prepared and the planting done with care, but the ritual act had to accompany it. It was unthinkable that there could be a crop on any other terms. Either without the other would surely fail. Marriage, conception, birth, illness, death—these, too, were occasions in which religion was one of the basic conditions. It was, for good or ill, involved in the struggle for social well-being.

Judaism has never lost the naive simplicity of this tribal faith.

In Judaism religion was never allowed to be divorced from the regulations of the sociolegal code and become limited to an emotion, or a quest of personal salvation, or a practice of ecclesiastical ceremony (says Rabbi David de Sola Pool). The establishment of just relations between capital and labor, between master and servant, between citizen and alien, between rich and poor, so repeatedly and explicitly called for in the Mosaic, prophetic, and rabbinic codes, is just as much an essential of the religion of Judaism as are the spiritual experiences with which religion is popularly identified. . . . Inevitably, therefore, the trend of Judaism is toward unifying human relationships with spiritual values. Characteristically, Judaism tends to evolve as its ideal human figure not the saint, who is often a secluded worldfleeing figure, but the one whom the Bible designates as "the righteous," *i.e.,* the just who moves in the world of men and loves his neighbor as himself.[1]

It was in this tradition that Christianity began. Jesus Himself, according to the biblical account, was more concerned with the righteousness and justice of God than with His gentleness. And the social implications of His teachings were exacting and stern. In spite of the other-worldliness of the Church before Constantine and the constant expectation of the return of the Christ in glory, there was a strong emphasis upon a sharing of worldly goods and upon gifts to the poor and the needy:

During the period of increasing barbarization of the provinces the bishop of the Christian community became more and more a person of great importance in each local center. He was the administrator of the vast system of charities and benevolences. Widows and orphans, the sick and infirm, the aged and unemployed, were cared for. The succor of those who were imprisoned for their faith during the period of persecution had developed into provision for ransoming of Christians made prisoners by barbarians. The burial of the indigent dead, the care of slaves, hospitality for strangers who were Christians, also assumed their place in the program of the Church. Both in the administration of these works of mercy and through gifts and bequests the church came to possess a great deal of property.[2]

These functions of the Church continued through the Middle Ages in the period of the Church's greatest wealth and power. The monastic movement played a large part. The Protestant Reformation, with its emphasis upon individualism, to an extent departed from the ancient tradition./And there was throughout the entire medieval period an absence in the Church of the Jewish prophetic concern for the correction of social evils./Alms-giving became a means to individual salvation. The curse of poverty and misery was accepted

---

[1] David de Sola Pool, "Judaism," *Religion and the Good Society,* Benson Y. Landis, editor, National Conference of Christians and Jews, New York, 1942, p. 16.

[2] L. B. Holsapple, *Constantine the Great,* Sheed & Ward, New York, 1942, p. 59.

as natural and inevitable. No thought was given to the removal of its causes. Piety and pity were one, and the Scriptural phrase, "The poor ye have always with you," became a declaration of dependence which no one cared to challenge.

Though sincere effort was made to care for the poor of Protestant parishes following the Reformation, it is fair to say that with the coming of Protestantism the secularization of social welfare began. The Pietistic movement in Lutheran Germany and among the Protestant sects in England, notably the Quakers, in some measure offset this trend. But, by and large, beginning with the breakup of feudalism, the destruction of the monasteries, and the formulation of the English Poor Law in 1601 with its emphasis upon repression of vagrancy, the placing of responsibility for relief upon the local community, and the development of the work test, the secularization of social welfare has steadily proceeded.

But we lose true perspective upon that process if we forget the long centuries in which, among primitive men, religion and tribal well-being were woven into a single close pattern of life, and the nearly twenty centuries in which, in Israel and under Christian rule, the Church centered, motivated, and controlled the care of the sick and the insane, of widows and orphans, the homeless, the hungry, the unemployable. Nor must we forget that even today the three major Western faiths, Catholic, Protestant, and Jewish, maintain many institutions of social welfare throughout the United States and the world.

Unfortunately, however, there has been no thorough listing and analysis of the scope and significance of this work, nor any satisfactory setting forth of what social work in the light of present needs and services in the whole field of humanitarian effort under public and private auspices, the churches and synagogues should be engaged upon.

As other papers in this volume will surely make clear, there are pronounced differences in the adequacy of the records in Catholic, Jewish, and Protestant social work. The annual *Official Catholic Directory* offers an impressive array of facts and figures. The *Jewish Social Work Year Book* representing a less unified constituency, cannot be so nearly precise. It should be remembered, however, that Jewish social work, though religious in inspiration and origin, is not administered under the jurisdiction of synagogues and temples. Protestantism, with its wide range of denominations and handicapped by the prevalent habit of vaguely considering as Protestant welfare all that is not Catholic or Jewish, is unable to give more than a rough estimate of its activities and accomplishments.

The National Council of the Churches of Christ in the United States of America deeply aware of this situation within Protestantism, sponsored in November, 1955, a nation-wide representative Conference on the Churches and Social Welfare. The Council's Division of Home Missions and Department of Social Welfare are especially concerned to get the essential facts about these activities as a basis for the shaping of church policies and plans. It is an indication of the size and scope of Protestant efforts in social welfare and the confused state of its record-keeping that for the 145,000 local churches of member denominations alone, with their more than 35,000,000 members, the gathering of these essential facts would involve the active cooperation of hundreds of people and would cost many thousands of dollars.

Fortunately some facts have been made available in roughly comparable form for the three major Western faiths, through the *Social Work Year Book* published as a rule biennially since 1929. Each volume contains articles on Catholic, on Jewish, and on Protestant social work. (It is fitting that in the 1951 and 1954 volumes the articles on Protestant social work are by F. Ernest Johnson, making a remarkable best of the bad bargain of inadequate statistics.) There is no doubt that, as with previous volumes, readers of these articles will be deeply impressed with the physical and financial proportions of these religiously related welfare organizations—hospitals, settlements, orphanages, schools, colleges, homes for the aged, work with immigrants and other under-privileged groups, work with migrants and the physically handicapped, relief and reconstruction overseas, family case-work and social education and action—all these activities revealing imagination and resourcefulness and a deep commitment to self-giving service. And alongside these specialized efforts and agencies of the churches must be placed the quiet charities practised within the membership of the churches themselves, the patient pastoral care and counseling, the families sustained through crisis and sorrow, the security that comes of shared faith and fellowship, the religious education of children and youth, and the provision of wholesome recreation.

But he whose task is to speak the prologue dare not for his life mouth in advance the speeches of the actors he introduces. And I am glad this is so, because my strongest personal interest is not in the recounting of facts present or past, impressive as these are, but in the effort to formulate what in the present and future is properly the place of religion in the field of human welfare. Let me, then, turn to this exciting and dangerous task of judgment and prophecy, rendered doubly hard by the radical and rapid changes which are occurring in the disordered world in which we live.

Thus far I have tried to indicate something of the history of the long partnership of religion and welfare, the scope and importance of their joint endeavors. Against this background, I want to offer for your critical consideration the two major issues to which I earlier referred—the relation of man to God and to government as these relations profoundly modify the present and future of the social outreach of organized religion in the United States, and doubtless elsewhere as well.

Of course I speak as a Protestant and out of very personal involvement and concern in what might be called the current trend in Protestant theology. But the issue is broader and deeper than the confines of any one creedal system, since it is basic to all philosophizing. Certainly no serious consideration of the relation of religion to human welfare can escape the question, "What is man's place in the universal scheme and his share and function in the fulfilment of his destiny?"

Even did your time and patience permit, I am not enough of a philosopher to deal significantly with this great issue. But I cannot escape the necessity of noting certain relations between some of the answers philosophers and theologians have given and man's efforts at human betterment.

The easy liberalism of the Social Gospel exalted man's knowledge, exaggerated his goodness, and led the youth of my day to look for the millennium around the corner. The disillusionment after the First World War was the more drastic on that account. The utopian idealism of a war to end war brought deeper discouragement after Versailles and the terrible years of the Depression. With the coming of World War II our youthful optimism was a fantastic memory, with its silly sense of power and of pride and its wide-eyed anticipations. It was inevitable that we should repent of our folly, admit our social failure, and confess the depth of our sinfulness and ignorance.

In the theology of crisis man renounced his pride and his presumption, his futile attempt to be Godlike in the control of his destiny, his sinfulness and powerlessness before God, and his need of God's grace for salvation. This was wholesome in the main, though extreme in some of its expressions. Had the crisis passed, its theology might well have gone with it. But with increasing confusion in international affairs, a deepened realization of the irreparable damage war had done, and a growing fear of atomic desolation in World War III, there was little on which to build sound optimism. The result has been that, with varying degrees of intensity, the theology of crisis has established itself as a truly significant emphasis in the religious thought of the world. Its strength in occupied Germany and in Japan underlines its affinity with critical social frustrations.

From the viewpoint of the relation between religion and human welfare, this theology is of great importance. Its effects have been profound but inconsistent. Among its adherents, God's design has replaced man's will, God's power and grace have revealed in contrast man's helplessness and sin. And it has become increasingly clear that this tends to negate the significance of human effort toward social betterment. Yet—and here lies the apparent inconsistency—from the time of Karl Barth's daring challenge to Nazism and the totalitarian state, there has been exemplified in these theological leaders an aggressive service in social causes. This may be in part an emotional compensation for the personal futility that theology logically induces. It is said by some to be a divine imperative to do what little a sinful "creature" can to be like his Creator. In some it seems to grow out of a deep conviction which must be shared, that God's love is inexhaustible and untiring, however great a man's sins may be. But, significant as this surely is, it remains doubtful that, at long last, a humility of spirit that takes the initiative from man and magnifies his sinfulness can provide the drive and devotion supplied by a faith in man's indestructible yearning after goodness and in God's glad use of man's abilities in the work God wills him to do.

And history denies that man is powerless to help himself. True, there is a vast amount of evil in the world and in the hearts of men. All that men have accomplished leaves us a long way from the Holy City. The going is hard, terrifyingly hard. No Utopia is anywhere in sight. But surely there is a sound reason for encouragement in the progress men have made. The history of social legislation in Europe and America—in penology, in child care, in health and housing, in education, in labor relations, in recreation—offers an impressive record of man's achievements in self-help. If it be held that the soul's salvation has nothing to do with its social environment and material condition, I cannot agree. I have seen too many eager youthful faces dulled and scarred and saddened, too many young dreams crushed out, by the injustice of poverty and discrimination, by established patterns of living sustained by custom more often than by evil design and surely susceptible of change.

Father James T. McDonnell, in stating the Catholic position, writes: "The protection of human dignity and the guarantee of decent standards of living have a direct bearing on the spiritual life of man as well as on his natural happiness." [3]

We have crudely over-estimated man's power and goodness, forgetting how weak and sinful we are. We have been quite blind to the social obstacles in traditionalism and fear of the new, in vested power interests, and in our lack of scientific knowledge and skills. Now we are ashamed of our strutting adolescent pride and what it cost our world in suffering. Now we are older and wiser. Our insights and our material resources have vastly multiplied. Can we not now safely and soberly reenlist as fellow workers under God,

[3] James T. McDonnell, *Social Work Year Book*, Russell Sage Foundation, 1947, p. 82.

deeply committed to our faith that the sinfulness of our society is not all of it innate in us and others like ourselves; that with knowledge of the facts and wise planning on the basis of facts, and with the creative use of some of the billions of dollars now spent each year in arming for destruction, we can help to build homes and neighborhoods and cities where decency and virtue are easier come by than filth and vice, and where men and women and little children will find the former more desirable to win and easier to keep, because the city is planned to make it so?

This is a dream of human welfare that cannot come true without our help. It is a dream so simple and so beautiful that only God working in us and in spite of us can make it fully a reality. The present low state of public morals, as reflected in political corruption, racketeering, and crime, certainly reinforces the conviction of man's sinfulness. The seeming indifference and irresponsibility of the men and women of our churches is due, I believe, less to personal involvement in these evils than to the loss of any strong conviction that much can be done about them or that God expects them to try. Has not the sincere humility that has dictated the conclusion that God has no need of man, been self-defeating in presuming to know God's mind and His desires? And does it not place a limitation upon God's power to say that the Creator cannot use His "creatures" as instruments of His will? To believe God gives man a share in the task of redemption is no more presumptuous, nor does it limit God's power.

So much for theology. Now let us turn earthward to study the relation of man to government in the field of welfare. Religiously-related social-welfare activity, in spite of its size and strength, is being crowded to the wall by two rivals, non-sectarian private welfare agencies and the Welfare State. With the development of Protestant sectarianism after the Reformation, the administration of charity became fragmented, necessitating the intervention of representatives of the community who themselves became practitioners.

As time passed, agencies evolved around differing types of need, and special knowledge and methods were accumulated that were beyond the time and energy of the priest and minister to acquire and use. It is significant that, although social work had its beginnings in the Church, the professional social worker was called into effective being by and for the secular welfare agencies. The result was that in many instances the church social worker was satisfied to substitute specifically religious emphasis and ability for the professional training which the social worker soon was expected to receive. And, conversely, the social worker in the secular agency tended to discount the contribution of religion. This is less often true than formerly—on both sides.[4]

But the more important problem is to determine the extent to which a church is justified in duplicating agency resources in any community in order to be sure that related religious needs of clients be met. There is no right answer for all situations, but economy and cooperation would seem to discredit overlapping. In most cities there are Catholic, Jewish, Protestant, and non-sectarian private agencies offering the same general types of service. As I have already suggested, there is a tendency to classify as Protestant clients all who are not clearly identified as belonging in another category. And it is becoming more and more the practise of sectarian hospitals and community centers to serve persons of other faiths. But non-sectarian agencies have in many areas of social welfare assumed a large share of the burden. Significant of the fading out of the antagonisms of the past generation is the fact that the *Yearbook of American Churches,* covering all faiths in the United States, regularly publishes a single alphabetized list of all national service agencies, social, civic, religious, of which well over half are non-sectarian.

But competition in well-doing presents the most serious problem when the voluntary agency confronts the tax-supported agency in its field of interest. It is apparent to all that in the modern state the government has already occupied much of the field of social welfare and will continue to do so. Long the competitor of the Church in well-doing (in Italy as early as the twelfth century there had been town hospitals managed by citizens and not by clergy), the state has now so far outstripped both the Church and private secular

---

[4] See Horace R. Cayton and Setsuko M. Nishi, *The Changing Scene: Current Trends and Issues,* National Council of Churches, New York, 1955, Chapter 13, pp. 160–168.

agencies as to threaten their continued existence in the field. In thirty-four urban areas in 1940 with a population of 17,200,000, of all current expenditures for health and welfare, as reported by the Children's Bureau, 90.1 per cent came from public funds, Federal, State, and local, and 9.9 per cent from private funds. In the relief and family welfare field 96 per cent of all funds were from public sources. At the lowest extreme 40.6 per cent of all funds for leisure-time activities were thus derived. Where current figures are available through Community Chests and Councils they indicate that the trend toward fuller public support is continuing.

It seems very likely that social welfare will become the almost exclusive function of the state. There are many dangers involved in this, it is true. But there is also much to be gained. Philanthropy, the love of man, can often be degrading to all concerned. Condescension calls attention to the social distance between class and class. Dependency is encouraged by generosity. Sentimentality drives out intelligence. And, although it is true that public charity may exhibit all these faults, there is the strong impression that private giving, especially when religiously motivated, is less objective and less impartial. Within limits, it is less embarrassing, more self-respecting, to receive aid from the public purse. For public education and for recreation in parks and playgrounds, the family is taxed according to its capacity and receives according to its needs. Here there is no sense of degradation. *Some* public hospitals have become reasonably free of this taint. Not so, however, with the more elemental needs. Although during the Depression to be on relief was so common as largely to be robbed of its stigma, yet to receive medical care, food, clothing, or shelter at public expense *is* to lose status in most neighborhoods. The reason is obvious. The need of these latter services indicates an inability to earn one's own living, as the need of education or recreation does not.

Although private giving has been so organized in the Community Chest as to become only slightly less obligatory than public taxation, the latter as a source of help is more impersonal and impartial, more nearly one's due and right, easier on one's self-respect. To exercise the privilege of giving freely to meet others' needs is often salutary and enjoyable. The payment of taxes under compulsion of law can never be a real substitute for this blessedness. Social security, sickness, and old-age insurance, subsidy for the nurture of children —these are inevitable in the modern state. It must be the duty of religion to give over much of its remaining charity, not to private secular agencies, but to the government. It must be the function of the churches generally so to exalt citizenship as to make the accept- ance of such a system welcome, and the payment of these taxes a glad sharing of the common burden.

There is at present a further serious limitation placed on the Church as an agency of social welfare. It is divided. Therefore any church which sets out to meet a social need divides the community. In simpler primitive societies there was but one creed and all ac- cepted it. There are few American towns where this is true today. By that one inescapable fact the Church is constrained to serve the needs of its own constituency (and then only in so far as they are not more economically met by other and secular agencies, especially those of government). A Protestant Church which, with no desire to proselytize, seeks to meet the social necessities of non-Protestants —or, it may be, of non-Baptists, is inevitably accused of "poaching." In a city of many churches no one of them can publicly inaugurate a community-wide service without antagonizing many others. In the field of welfare, to organize the community is not a proper function for the Church. It must share with others in the effort. It ought not openly to initiate and control it.

But in these small and closely integrated groups of churches and synagogues lies a potential contribution to human welfare which may more than compensate for their divisiveness and provide an antidote to the deadly poison of dictatorship which may so easily possess the Welfare State. Democracy thrives best in the small community. The bigness of American cities threatens to make us all mass men with no inner drive to keep us from yielding to the outer compulsions of press and politics, radio and television, lobbies and pressure groups, and their propaganda. Mass men are the easy dupes of dictators. In our complex American society no agency other than government can possibly carry the burden of welfare. That burden will continue heavy until at last the science of social planning and of social control frees us from the clumsy injustices of our present system.

The neighborhood group in church or synagogue, bound by a common faith and by shared interests, is the readiest and most numerous means of developing intelligent citizen interest and participation in community problems and in community service. National committees or departments or conferences in all of the three major Western faiths have become organized to promote social service and action. These are regularly listed as among their welfare activities. But few of the many local Protestant churches I have known show any realization of the social power lying unused within their membership. There is no effective means of keeping the vast machinery of modern public welfare from political and economic domination of the citizen, except the citizen himself. And to his task he must be educated and organized and inspired.

Here, if we but recognize and use it, is religion's greatest opportunity for effective social welfare in our generation. Here in the local church whose fellowship holds, in the common loyalty of faith, groups alert and informed and active, some in one sphere of community effort, some in another, are the means of guiding and controlling public welfare as servant and not as master. Here, too, stimulated by a theology of faith in God and man, is the chance once more to put religion to work at the heart of American life to the strengthening of American Democracy.

And now I have done. I have tried to set the stage and speak the prologue for the actors who are to succeed me. Crudely sketched before you here is the outline of religion's early and developing concerns with human welfare, from prehistory through Israel's inspired leadership to its fruition in the later efforts of synagogue and church, through the Reformation and the resulting secularization of religious social welfare, to the present with its basically conflicting theologies and its competitions in well-doing, and the threat of the Welfare State, with its inevitable though partial victory over voluntary welfare effort. Finally, I have tried to throw out a challenge to make of organized religions in America a powerful means to the control of statism and bureaucracy in the service of the people, and thus restore religion to its rightful place at the heart of American community life.

II

PROTESTANT SOCIAL WORK TODAY

BY

ALMON R. PEPPER

Director, Department of Christian Social Relations,
Protestant Episcopal National Council

For the purposes of our presentation and discussion it is necessary for us to have a common mind about our subject. We need to know what we mean by Protestant and within this context what we mean by social work.

Protestant means a lot of different things to different people. We will simplify our problem if for the purposes of this paper we limit our consideration to the social work of those churches which are cooperating through the National Council of the Churches of Christ in the United States of America. This means thirty church bodies, among which are the Lutheran, Methodist, Presbyterian, Baptist, Episcopal, Congregational-Christian, Disciples of Christ, Russian, Greek, and Serbian Eastern Orthodox Churches, and by special provision, the Salvation Army. It includes also such agencies as are directly related to the National Council or to local councils of churches.

The Protestant social work with which we shall be concerned is related to these churches in varying degrees of control, supervision, or traditional ties.

First, there is the agency which is the complete child of the church or some official branch or jurisdiction of the church. It is recognized by both the church and the social agency that the latter is responsible to the church authorities and is an agent of theirs. This type of relationship is rather recent in origin, and the number of agencies so related is comparatively small. Often this type of agency does not have a board of trustees or managers, but is governed by a committee responsible to the larger body.

Second, there is the agency which, by its own constitution and bylaws, defines a variety of relationships with a particular church. It may provide that its board of trustees or some percentage of them must be members of the particular church body, or that the chief officer of the church shall be the presiding officer of the agency. Sometimes the trustees are required to be members of a particular church, but this is not required of the board of managers. In some instances, it is required that the religious services of the agency shall be according to the rites of a particular church. A chief distinction between this and our first type of church-related agency is that the degree of relatedness is determined by the agency alone, with no reciprocal acknowledgment of the relationship defined by the church.

A third type of relationship is that brought about by traditional and loyalty ties, but nowhere defined or required. This often makes for a very close and happy relationship between church and agency. But often, too, in times of change or adversity, it makes for serious trouble. Many social agencies in our American communities which are now thought of as non-sectarian had their beginnings under these undefined and vaguely Protestant auspices. It is also true that some of the churches had a policy of inaugurating social services as pioneering to meet new or growing needs, with the intention of having them continued under general community auspices.

A fourth category includes the social services developed by local or state councils of churches, and, in the case of Church World Service, by the National Council of Churches.

In summary, any survey of "Protestant" social work will include agencies having these several types of relatedness to the churches. At the present time a variety of forces would seem to be encouraging the agencies and the churches to draw closer together. Among these forces we would note the following:

a. An increasing recognition by the churches and the agencies that their services are integral parts of a single purpose.

b. Development by the churches of a more inclusive interest in the people of the community. Social work is not something extraneous, but a normal part of the service of the Church.

c. The need of social agencies, faced with ever larger and more impersonal communities, for closer ties with church groups which can interpret and personalize their work.

d. The increased sharpness of sectarian patterns in community life.

e. Increased costs of operation of social services and the necessity of seeking official church support, both directly and by sponsorship.

Types of Services Offered by Protestant Social Work

Every type of social work would be found in a detailed catalogue of the services offered by the churches or in their name. It is natural that this should be the case because of religious concern for the welfare of individuals and of families. In order to catch the full flavor of this wide concern we need to review the existing types of services:

1. *Child-Care Agencies.* These were some of the earliest agencies to be established and are among the most numerous at present. Orphanages were established early in most of the large cities on the Eastern seaboard. Some homes for children had their beginnings following epidemics, and others after the War between the States. Many of these homes have now added foster-home placement services, while others have given up congregate care entirely and now provide full case-work services. In recent years a few agencies have come into being with the initial purpose of providing case-work service for children and youth. Some of the agencies are licensed adoption agencies, and a few of them provide service to children with mental and emotional handicaps.

2. *Services for the Aged.* Homes for the Aged are among the most numerous of church-sponsored agencies. They are usually restricted to members of the particular denomination operating the Home. In recent years some of these Homes have added foster-home placement to their programs, and subsidies and case-work services to needy aged people in their own homes. Some churches have developed

counseling services for the aged. Many parish churches now offer facilities for leisure-time activities to the elderly people in their neighborhoods. It is interesting to note that some of the Eastern Orthodox churches, with membership made up wholly of one nationality group, have benevolent societies whose sole purpose is to care for members in their old age. Among all the churches at the present time, services for the aged are receiving greater attention than service for any other group.

3. *Hospitals.* Church-related hospitals range from small institutions in rural or remote areas to some of the largest and best of the private hospitals in the country. They may include all of the specialized services of modern hospitals maintained under any auspices. Many of them have schools of nursing. A characteristic feature of church hospitals is a chapel which is an integral part of the institution, with regular religious ministry usually through a full-time chaplain.

4. *Community Centers.* Churchmen were among the early sponsors of the settlement house movement in this country. In addition to the establishment of settlements in the technical sense, they also developed neighborhood houses and various forms of group work. In the early days these centers were usually in areas removed from parish churches. More recently, because of changing populations and changing attitudes and motives in the churches, they are being more closely related to the fabric as well as the program of the parish church. This is especially the case of many inner-city churches which find themselves confronted with vast new populations, many strangers to religion or to its manifestations through the old established churches. To meet this challenge and opportunity, group activities and other social services are being experimented with as a means of serving the people and the community.

5. *Seamen's Work.* Some of the American churches having strong ties with European churches whose sons and daughters served in the merchant ships of their nation established homes and services for these people while they were in American ports. Other churches, seeing the plight of seamen while in port, established such services for general humanitarian reasons. It should be noted that religious

bodies showed an interest in the welfare of seamen long before there was any general community concern.

6. *Services for Migrants.* Welfare services for migrants are usually established and supported by interdenominational agencies. They offer a variety of services to migrant workers as they move around the country: worship services and religious ministry, recreation, health services, educational opportunities, and emergency relief.

7. *Family Case-work.* In many an American community the present family service society had its earliest beginnings in a simple relief service established by members of Protestant churches. Today there are only a few church-related family service agencies. In less formal terms, however, case-work and counseling are offered to families and individuals in a variety of settings—as a service of parish churches or regional jurisdictions, through councils of churches, and as part of the service of City Mission and Inner Mission Societies.

8. *Chaplaincy Services and Pastoral Counseling.* Religious ministry in hospitals and prisons and pastoral counsel to people with special personal or family problems are normal parts of the ministry of the churches; but they are treated in a paper on Protestant social work because the special settings in which they operate may give them a high degree of social-work content. The services of ministers and priests of the churches are made available to many public and private institutions on the initiative of the churches themselves. Increasingly, Federal, State, and to a lesser degree, city authorities provide budget and facilities for the employment of official chaplains in their hospitals and prisons. Following the example of Federal agencies, many State and municipal authorities are now requiring specialized clinical training for these chaplains. To meet these special requirements, for chaplaincy services as well as for their responsibilities in pastoral counseling, an increasing number of the clergy are attending schools of social work or clinical training courses in pastoral care.

9. *Social Education and Social Action.* Social action shows itself more readily at the regional and national levels than in local congre-

gations; and more readily in interdenominational associations than in those of individual denominations. Some of the most effective work has been done in race relations and housing, and in connection with Displaced Persons legislation and the problems of world order. Interfaith cooperation is most readily carried on in this type of social work.

10. *World Relief and Resettlement of Refugees.* Most of the Protestant and Eastern Orthodox churches have their own programs of world relief and resettlement of refugees, but they are based upon a program which centers in Church World Service of the National Council of Churches and in the Department of Interchurch Aid and Resettlement of Refugees of the World Council of Churches. These programs include practically every aspect of overseas relief and rehabilitation work. In sponsoring and resettling a family of refugees many a local congregation has gained a new insight into the need for and practice of social work.

11. *Miscellaneous Services.* The pressure of human needs has caused the churches to develop a variety of other services—counseling and protective services in children's and family courts; clinics; homes for the blind, the deaf, and the mentally disturbed; rehabilitation centers; and rest homes.

It should be noted that these services are not established everywhere that need shows itself. Of some types of service there are only a few examples, while other types, such as child care and services for the aged, are general. This indicates that, while the welfare of people is a primary concern of *Christianity,* the establishment and maintenance of social agencies is a secondary concern of the *churches.* But it should also be noted that in many a small town or rural setting it is the churches, more than any other association of men, that bring new services into being. Moreover, during the war, it was the churches that gave leadership in developing social services in new industrial areas. It was the churches and synagogues that carried the major responsibility in the resettlement of Displaced Persons and that will do the same for the refugees under the present legislation.

Central Organization for Protestant Social Work

Until comparatively recent years the social work of the churches was chiefly a matter of local concern. The several denominations had central boards for missions, but corresponding concern for social service developed later.

Central Denominational Programs for social service developed along with national strategy and promotion in all fields of church work. At the present time most of the denominations have national and regional departments concerned with various phases of social welfare. The names of these departments and the content of their programs are not the same in any two denominations though a trend toward uniformity can be noted.

In some of the churches the central agency is promotional, educational, and standard-setting in nature. Other churches have set up central boards which support, control, or supervise the social services of the denomination. These central boards usually offer their agencies the following services: regional and national conferences, surveys, recruiting and placement services, standard-setting, and some form of accreditation.

Interdenominational Programs. Interestingly enough, the cooperative movement among the churches has perhaps done as much as any other force to make the several church bodies become centrally conscious of their social services.

State and local councils of churches have brought the social agencies of the churches together for conference and cooperation. It is in these settings that an idea of "Protestant strategy" in social work has developed. Under the influence of these local interdenominational councils, new coordination of services has developed, as well as mergers of agencies and the establishment of new services.

On behalf of the cooperating denominations, these local councils have developed central information and referral services, and a wide range of direct services which vary in different communities. These services are usually financed in part by the local Community Fund as a counterpart to support given to the other major faiths. In New

York the nature of this local interdenominational cooperation and coordination is seen in the program and activities of the Federation of Protestant Welfare Agencies and those of the Protestant Council.

But the chief center of cooperation in Protestant social welfare is the National Council of Churches. Through its Division of Christian Life and Work and the Division of Home Missions, two of its major Divisions, the National Council encompasses nearly every phase of social work known to the constituent churches and has added some new ones on their behalf.

A listing of some of the current activities of these National Council Divisions through their departments and committees will indicate the nature and scope of Protestant social welfare.

I. *Division of Christian Life and Work*. Special concerns for social work show themselves in the programs of the several departments as follows:

A. *Department of Social Welfare*

1. The Church Conference of Social Work is held annually as an associate member of the National Conference of Social Work.

2. The Christian Social Welfare Associates is a new organization which coordinates the interests of two former associations. The Associates sponsor and plan for the Church Conference of Social Work, publish a journal, *"Christian Social Welfare,"* and act as a clearinghouse for personnel placement.

3. The Department has been making a study of all social welfare activities of constituent bodies of the National Council. It participated with the Division of Home Missions in sponsoring the 1955 National Conference on the Churches and Social Welfare.

4. The Department holds with some regularity national and regional conferences on child care and services to the aged.

5. The Department is actively interested in recruiting and training personnel for social work. It is a charter member of the Council for Social Work Education.

B. *Department of Pastoral Services*

1. This Department recruits and clears all Protestant Chaplains

for Federal prisons and has helped to develop the high standards established for this service.

2. Through the Department the American Protestant Hospital Association cooperates with the National Council of Churches in the study of religious work in the hospital, with particular emphasis on the work of the Chaplain. The Department also cooperates with the Association in planning its annual meetings.

C. Other departments of the Division of Christian Life and Work, such as the Department of Racial and Cultural Relations, the Department of the Church and Economic Life, and the Department of International Affairs, devote major attention to social education and community action in their respective fields of interest.

II. *Division of Home Missions.* In this Division there is active interest in the welfare of migrants, American Indians, Latin Americans, and other minority groups.

III. The General Department of United Church Women also supports various social programs in these fields.

IV. *The Central Department of Church World Service* is engaged in a broad field that includes important social services.

A. In cooperation with the authorized representatives of the Roman Catholic and Jewish communities, Church World Service actively favored passage of the Refugee Resettlement Act of 1953, intended to admit about 200,000 refugees to the United States. As of this time the churches related to Church World Service have secured more than 25,000 "assurances," covering 50,000 of these refugees.

B. The relief and rehabilitation programs of the churches, coordinated through Church World Service, extend into all parts of the free world.

Motivation and Trends in Protestant Social Work

It is no easy matter to generalize about the motives involved in the pattern of Protestant social work. The agencies came into being under a variety of auspices, at different times in the history of our country, and in answer to a variety of social needs. Today, these agencies are governed by a variety of boards and are variously related to the churches. It is inevitable therefore that there should be a wide range of motives involved in their operation. Some were established for humanitarian reasons, some as missionary and evangelistic programs, and some as demonstration pilot projects.

Permeating all these secondary motives is the basic belief of all the agencies that they are carrying out a requirement of their religion. Some will think of this in solely Christian terms. Others see it as a manifestation of the longer Judeo-Christian reference through the life and teachings of Jesus.

The full picture of motivation may be brought up to date by consideration of some of the present-day trends in the social work of the Protestant churches.

1. Increasingly the churches are seeing their social work, not as something separate and "different," but as an expression of the normal ministry of the Church carried on in special settings.[1] The reverse side of this picture shows that the special competences of social workers, psychiatrists, and social scientists are being increasingly used in the ministry of parish churches.

2. The social work of the churches is giving more attention to the total needs of man, with greater emphasis upon the ways in which "religious therapy" can assist in meeting the spiritual and emotional needs of the "clients."

3. The agencies themselves and the churches are seeking closer ties and working relationships with each other. This is a natural result of the trends noted above. It shows itself at the local, regional, and national levels.

4. Where there are strong State or local councils of churches there is an increase of association between the social agencies of the several churches, and a new sense of their corporate responsibilities and of their opportunities for working with social agencies and social workers.

5. Out of this local sense of corporate responsibility the local councils of churches will be encouraged to develop new services on behalf of the cooperating churches.

6. The new sense of common responsibility and of corporate strength developing at the grass roots will influence, and be influenced by, the same trend in common purpose being developed through the activities of the churches in the National Council of Churches.

7. All of this should produce more new services and a strengthening of old services, improvement in the standards of social work done, and marked progress in the development of religious therapy.

8. These trends will lead to a more united front for the social service agencies of the Protestant churches; they may also sharpen the sectarian aspects of social work in many communities—a prospect which arouses mixed emotions in many quarters.

Conclusion

Any attempt to describe the social welfare program of the Protestant churches has been handicapped by the lack of basic statistical and descriptive material, and by the wide range of tradition and practice of the churches. In November, 1955, a National Conference on the Churches and Social Welfare, sponsored by departments of the National Council of Churches, was held in Cleveland. A statistical survey has emerged which will correct this deficiency. This conference may also have marked a turning-point in the social work of the church bodies constituent of the National Council, by making them conscious of the extent of their own services and the potentialities of combined and coordinated programs.

We can be sure that social work and social welfare services will be a major concern of the Christian churches as long as we live in a free society, because basic to the Christian religion is an abiding concern for the health and wholeness of body, soul, and mind of the individual, and for the common good of the society in which he lives. For religion not to be concerned about these matters would mean its loss of relatedness to life itself. For the Christian churches this would mean that they had turned against their Lord Who said, "I came that they might have life, and have it more abundantly."

III

CATHOLIC CHARITIES IN THE UNITED STATES —BACKGROUND AND PRESENT OUTLOOK

BY

RIGHT REVEREND MONSIGNOR JOHN O'GRADY

Secretary, National Conference of Catholic Charities

It is impossible to discuss the history and programs of Catholic Charities without reference to the so-called "old" immigration tide between 1840 and 1870 and the later tide during the two decades prior to the First World War. All the developments in Catholic Charities during the first period grew largely out of the problems of the immigrants and especially those who settled in the large urban centers. Even the problems of those who followed the lure of the free land in the West had their reflections in Catholic Charities programs. Lack of adequate farm backgrounds and of resources caused many of the immigrants to fail to adjust to the difficult conditions confronting the pioneers on the land and they were compelled to return to the Middle Western or Eastern cities. The efforts of the pioneer Catholic leaders of St. Louis, for example, were devoted for the most part to aiding Irish settlers who had failed to adjust to conditions in the newly developed State of Kansas.

Irish immigration from 1840 to 1860 presented many difficult social problems. As this writer has pointed out:

There was nothing planned or systematic about the great tide of Irish emigration. It was just a mad, headlong rush of a people from a dungeon in which they were exposed to slow and painful death. Where they were going they knew not. They were just seeking nature's first escape from suffering. The dangers of the new land and the journey thereto could not be any more real than those to which they had been exposed at home.[1]

Irish emigration in 1847 doubled that of any previous year and reached a total of 105,536. By 1851 it had reached its crest with 221,253.

Another quotation gives a vague picture of the sufferings of the Irish immigrants on their way over the North Atlantic:

During the four last months of 1853, 312 vessels arrived at New York from European ports, with 96,950 passengers. Of these vessels 47 were visited by cholera, and 1,933 passengers died at sea.[2]

To the sufferings that the Irish encountered on their voyage must be added the hardships they faced in American cities. Large numbers of them died in epidemics in the Eastern and Middle Western cities. This left numberless children without parents and without homes. It is only in terms of these epidemics that we can understand the establishment of such a great number of Catholic child-caring institutions between 1840 and 1875.

Organizing the Care of Needy Children

The parishes in which the immigrants lived made heroic efforts at first to take care of the children rendered homeless by epidemics or other causes. They soon found, however, that they could not cope with the problem, and, therefore, they appealed for assistance to the religious communities of women that had already been established in the United States. Among these, of course, the Sisters of Charity stood out most prominently. This community was established at Emmitsburg, Maryland, in 1809. During the early years the Sisters' basic interest was the education of the children of the original Catholic settlements in Philadelphia, Maryland, and Kentucky. Their first institutions were a combination of boarding school, day school,

---

[1] John O'Grady, *Catholic Charities in the United States: History and Problems,* National Conference of Catholic Charities, Washington, 1931, p. 39.

[2] *Report of the Select Committee of the Senate of the United States on the Sickness and Mortality on Board Emigrant Ships,* Washington, D.C., 1854, p. 9.

and orphanage. They accepted some dependent and neglected children as a part of their educational program. As the tide of Irish immigration developed, the Sisters of Charity were called upon to establish orphanages in New York, Philadelphia, Washington, Baltimore, Albany, Buffalo, St. Louis, and Boston.

There is another factor to be kept in mind in studying the history of Catholic Charities in the United States. During the years following the French Revolution all Europe, and especially France and Germany, experienced a Catholic revival. There is scarcely a period in the history of the Church more fruitful in the foundation of new religious communities than that between 1800 and 1860. To this period one can trace the origin of some of the best known religious communities of women in the United States. Catholic leaders in the United States anxiously appealed to these new communities to come to their rescue in dealing with the immigration tide to this country. These Sisterhoods did not necessarily have an institutional background, so that it cannot be said in any general way that the large institutional programs for children developed by the Church in the United States represented a European pattern. It would be more nearly correct to say that when the European Sisterhoods arrived they found an institutional pattern already set up. This was probably the best that could have been done in view of the large number of children deprived of their parents by the epidemics that spread over the cities in which the immigrants had settled.

In evaluating the vast institutional program set up for the care of Catholic children between 1840 and 1875, one must keep in mind the structure of the Catholic parish during this period. Most of the parishes represented struggling immigrant settlements. An adequate priesthood had not yet been developed. It was too early to expect a native priesthood and European countries were hard pressed in meeting their own needs.

The German immigrants who settled in American cities encountered many of the same problems as the Irish. They, too, died in large numbers in epidemics in cities like Rochester, Buffalo, and Cincinnati. They were just as anxious as the Irish to protect the religious interests of their children. Coming from a different background, they placed greater emphasis on lay participation in the work of their children's institutions. They aimed to have a large lay membership from which their boards of directors were elected. They regarded their institutions as cooperatives that protected their members against the hazards of premature death.

The patterns developed by the Irish and the German immigrants in the care of their children were followed by other national groups, such as the Italians, Poles, Czechs, and sometimes also the Lithuanians. In other words, the institutions of Catholic Charities became largely the expression of the interest of the different ethnic groups in their own children. To a limited degree this pattern still survives, but in another generation very little probably will be left of it.

During the decade 1870 to 1880, voluntary organizations, like the New York Children's Aid Society, the Children's Mission to Children in Boston, and the Home for Little Wanderers also in Boston, had a great deal of responsibility for the removal of children from the local county and town almshouses. This presented a new opportunity and a new challenge. At that time the States and local communities were confronted with the problem of caring for large numbers of children who had been separated from their own homes. In the development of their programs the issue between those who believed in institutional care and those who believed in placing children in foster homes was joined. The large child-caring agencies believed that they could find homes for the children who were removed from the almshouses. The representatives of Catholic Charities were afraid that the placing of these children through agencies of other denominations would mean the loss of the faith of the children.

One of the most significant studies of that period was that made by Commissioner Letchworth of the New York State Board of Charities.[3] Commissioner Letchworth expressed the view that the children of the immigrants should be placed in institutions or agencies of their own religious faith. This report brought the discussion in the State to a head and really established in New York State a

[3] William P. Letchworth, *Homes for Homeless Children*, transmitted to the Legislature with the Annual Reports of the New York State Board of Charities, January, 1876.

pattern providing for the fullest use by local governments of the existing organizations of their own faith in the care of children. In a number of other States (*e.g.,* Illinois, Pennsylvania, Maryland, Michigan, and California) similar arrangements were made. Some States established State homes for children which in time were destined to become largely child-placing agencies. Other States, Massachusetts being the first, began to establish their own child-placing programs.

The issue as to the purchase of care for children from voluntary organizations operating on a religious basis was still very much under debate in the '80s and '90s. At the New York State Constitutional Convention in 1893, it was more or less the consensus that the prevailing practise of using voluntary organizations under religious auspices on the local level should be continued. The purchase of service by government from voluntary organizations has remained somewhat a moot question. It has been constantly in debate in a number of States throughout the country. Since the problems of child care have become more complex through the years, because of the interest in specialized care for many types of children, it has become increasingly difficult for governmental agencies properly to discharge all their responsibilities for the care of children without making the fullest use of the resources of voluntary organizations.

Throughout the 1880s, there was a good deal of discussion regarding the limitations of child-caring institutions. They were criticized especially because they did not have any follow-up of the children after their discharge. They were accused also of breaking up homes unnecessarily. It was to meet this criticism that the Catholic Home Bureau of New York was established by the St. Vincent de Paul Society in 1898. This was a significant step in the evolution of our present programs of Catholic Charities. It marked the beginning of systematic child-placing under Catholic auspices. In the course of the years it exercised an important influence in Catholic child care.

The seed planted by the Catholic Home Bureau of New York gradually took root. In 1903, under the leadership of Francis Fay, Newark set up a similar agency, the New Jersey Catholic Children's

Home Society; then came the Little Children's Aid Society of San Francisco in 1907. These were followed by child-placing societies in Washington, Detroit, Chicago, and Philadelphia.

In setting up child-placing agencies under Catholic auspices the leaders of the St. Vincent de Paul Society hoped to overcome the isolation of Catholic institutions. These new agencies, they thought, would bring the institutions into closer contact with the American community. As a matter of fact, however, the broadening of the programs of child-caring institutions was much more difficult than the St. Vincent de Paul members had anticipated. The work of the child-placing agencies was thought to be a threat to the institutions, many of which felt that the St. Vincent de Paul members were lining up with their other critics.

In 1902, Catholic leaders began to recognize the serious plight of large numbers of Catholic children cared for by governmental organizations. This movement, which began in Boston in 1902, led to the establishment of the Catholic Charitable Bureau whose basic purpose was to follow up with children cared for by the State Board of Minor Wards. This pattern was later developed in other cities. It cannot be said, however, that this plan has been entirely satisfactory. It has not been possible generally to establish on any extensive basis the type of follow-up that is necessary to preserve the religious faith of Catholic children under governmental auspices.

The providing of adequate religious programs for Catholic children under the care of governmental agencies also presented difficult problems. For those cared for in institutions it required adequate chaplain service. While some progress has been made in this area, a great deal more remains to be done. The Church is continuously confronted with a lack of priests to provide adequate religious services for Catholic children in public institutions. The same is true of public hospitals, including mental hospitals and in fact all public institutions, as well as a considerable number of Catholic institutions. There is not as yet sufficient recognition of the specialized type of Catholic chaplain service needed in all public institutions. Nor is there sufficient recognition of the fact that this service calls for special training. So far the only approach to this situation appears to be an in-service training program.

It would be practically impossible to provide a program of highly specialized services for Catholic children under governmental agencies in boarding or free homes. Services for these children must be virtually the same as for children cared for in their own homes. There needs, however, to be a special sensitivity on the part of parish schools and parish organizations generally to the problems presented by these children. So many times there has been a tendency to regard them as "charity children." Fortunately, this situation is gradually changing as the teachers in the schools become more sensitive to the problems involved.

Catholic Charities and Protective Care

Catholic Charities through the years has shown a considerable interest in juvenile delinquency. Local Catholic agencies have close contact with juvenile courts in many of the large centers. They collaborate with the courts in making plans for the care of children appearing in the courts. This contact has made Catholic Charities aware of the needs of Catholic children who face this ordeal. It has helped develop a new attitude on the part of Catholic institutions dealing with juvenile delinquents. These institutions have to a degree become more sensitive to the needs of the children. We are referring especially to the institutions operated by the Good Shepherd Sisters. There are in all some sixty-two such institutions. The standards of care in these institutions have changed very considerably in the past ten years. An increasing number of Good Shepherd Sisters are being trained in the fields of social work and psychology. They are participating in the discussions and workshops sponsored by the National Conference of Catholic Charities. To an increasing degree the Sisters are beginning to consult the best available technicians in regard to their programs. The work of the Good Shepherd Sisters today, on the whole, is one of the most significant parts of the entire American community program for the care of adolescent girls presenting behavior problems.

Some progress has been made by a few of the Good Shepherd homes in the evaluation of their own programs. They are beginning to study more carefully the whole question of their relationship and attitude toward the girls under their care. They are making their programs more flexible. They are giving the girls an opportunity to participate in regular community programs. It is expected that in the not distant future this group of institutions, with the aid of the best expert counsel, may be able to make more self-studies. This will be advantageous, as outside leadership will always have certain limitations in dealing with the problems presented by these institutions.

The years immediately following the Civil War saw a great interest on the part of Catholic leaders in the care of delinquent boys. During those years and up to 1890, institutions for delinquent boys were established under Catholic auspices in many cities in the United States. Today very few of these institutions remain. However, we still have a few institutions in this field that are making a significant contribution. Like the homes of the Good Shepherd, these institutions are beginning to study their own problems. One of them at least, Saint Anthony's Home in Cleveland, has been promoting neighborhood organization among Catholic groups to deal with boys presenting behavior problems.

It is the hope of leaders in Catholic Charities that in the future Catholic institutions caring for children away from their own homes will become more specialized—that they will concentrate their efforts on children requiring group care, or some form of specialized care, and that they will become an integral part of community programs for the care of children.

Beginning about 1890, Catholic leaders and organizations in certain cities became interested in the settlement movement. They were influenced by the programs of settlements like Hull House in Chicago, Henry Street Settlement in New York City, and others of a similar character. Catholic interest, however, was essentially a protective interest. The settlements set up under Catholic auspices aimed to reach the new immigrants who were not being fully reached by the existing parish organizations of the Church. Catholics generally had a good deal of suspicion about the influence of the activities of the non-sectarian settlements on the new immigrants. In the Catholic settlements, which were very small compared with the large non-sectarian settlements, there was emphasis on recreation programs for children and to a degree also for adults. There was also great emphasis on catechetical work for children.

During the First World War and the years immediately following there was a new interest in settlement work which came to be called "group work" under Catholic auspices in various communities in the United States. These group-work organizations still remain. In some places they are active and wide-awake but in other places their programs have become somewhat stereotyped. For the most part these programs, like the programs of settlements as a whole, tend to deal with special segments of the community rather than the whole community. Generally speaking, they do not seem to be as conscious as they might be of the forces at work in the disorganized areas of our cities. They have not as yet caught sufficiently the spark that is necessary to mobilize the people in these areas to help themselves in dealing with their own problems.

Many people are raising the question whether the settlements whose present programs reflect the thinking of another age can make a real contribution to the disorganized neighborhoods of today. They point out that the settlements are so busy maintaining their buildings and the programs which they have been offering through the years that they have little time left to study and to work on the problems of disorganized neighborhoods. In fact, the question is raised whether the personnel of present-day settlements lends itself to the type of program that is needed in these areas. However, we should not abandon hope of putting a new front on our settlements. We cannot discard all the institutions set up in another generation. We should rather aim to inspire them with that spirit of a Christian neighborhood in which people think and plan for themselves, in which people try to solve their own problems.

Care for the Aging and Chronically Ill

For many years the Catholic Church has had a number of religious communities of women devoted exclusively to institutional care of the aging. Among these are the Little Sisters of the Poor, the Carmelite Sisters for the Aged and Infirm, and the Sisters of Charity of Providence. The Little Sisters of the Poor have the largest number of homes for the aging, in all fifty-one. The Carmelite Sisters, more recently organized in 1929, now have twenty-three institutions for the aging.

In his history of Catholic Charities, the author pointed to the significant contribution made by Catholic institutions for the care of the aged.[4] At that time the "institution" offered the one ray of hope for the aging who were unable to care for themselves in their own homes. It was more or less assumed then that the ordinary aging could take care of themselves through their own savings or through the aid given by their children. This was largely true until the early '30s. When the author made his study on the aging for the Health and Old-Age Insurance Commission of Ohio in 1919, there was very little interest in the major problems of the aging. Beginning about that time, considerable interest was aroused throughout the United States in what was known as old-age pension. This was set forth as an effort to remove the dependent aging from the almshouses. Very little interest was aroused by the figures that the author published in 1919 about the influence of machinery in shortening the working life of the aging and also about the fact that a considerable sector of the aging were unable to save sufficient to take care of them during their last years. It was only during the years of the Depression that the American people began to understand the problem of the aging in its larger perspective.

When the Social Security Act was being considered by the Congress in 1935, the problems that stood out most prominently were those of the aging and of the unemployed. Therefore the Congress passed with very little debate the Social Security Act providing for these two groups.

In 1935, as in 1919, we found that people who had studied the problem of the aging approached it from two different angles. There were those who wanted to regard it as a problem of dependency and those who wanted to regard it as an industrial problem to be approached through a contributory system of Old-Age and Survivors

[4] O'Grady, *op. cit.*

Insurance. It was virtually agreed that the long-range approach should be the social insurance approach. However, due to immediate conditions and especially to the large number of aging receiving relief, it was considered necessary for the Federal government to provide grants-in-aid to the States for the care of the aging who did not have the opportunity to accumulate the necessary credits under Old-Age Insurance. It was believed that in time Federal aid to the States for Old-Age Assistance could be discontinued or reduced to a minimum when there was universal coverage under Old-Age Insurance.

In considering the place of our institutions for the aging in a general program for the aged today, one finds a situation much different from that of 1935. Now we have some 7,500,000 people receiving Old-Age Insurance benefits, in about 5,000,000 families, while we still have approximately 2,500,000 people receiving Old-Age Assistance under that Federal-State program. In addition to the governmental programs, we have a great many private programs built up by collective bargaining between employers and employees, and company retirement plans otherwise instituted. Altogether old-age benefits under all programs, apart from the older types of insurance, probably reach some 12,000,000 people.

Governmental and voluntary programs providing economic security for the aging raise many questions today as to the place of institutional care in the larger perspective. We not only have to evaluate the place of institutions in relation to the economic benefits that are provided for the aging, but we also have to evaluate them in terms of employment opportunities for the aging. We find that a majority of at least the male workers continue in gainful employment up to the age of seventy. We find, moreover, a great increase in the life expectancy of the aging. Since 1900 the life expectancy has been increased from forty-seven years to over sixty-nine years at the present time. This increase in longevity has left us with more people in the higher age brackets. This, of course, has a tendency to increase the incidence of chronic disease.

We find that the number of aging people cared for in institutions at the present time is only about three per cent of all the aging. This limitation of institutional facilities in relation to the increased volume of chronically ill raises some questions as to the basic function of the institutions. The general attitude today is that the institutions are designed to serve the need of a carefully selected group who cannot be provided for in any other way. In the selection of those for whom institutional facilities should be made available we must think of institutions in relation to other facilities. More recent studies have not borne out all our fears about the breakdown of family responsibility. We find that the great majority of the aging want to remain in their own homes or in the homes of relatives. We know, moreover, that a number of our Catholic institutions, as well as institutions operated by other religious denominations, are giving careful thought to ways and means of maintaining home life for the aging. They are giving increasing attention to the possibility of finding families who are willing to take aged people into their own homes.

For all practical purposes, therefore, institutions for the aging to-day are regarded as facilities for the care of those who cannot take care of themselves; therefore they are rapidly becoming nursing homes in which guests can receive nursing care on a twenty-four hour basis.

Problems Facing Catholic Charities in Dealing with the Aging and Chronically Ill

1. The first and most important concern of Catholic Charities in dealing with the aging and chronically ill is stimulation of interest in this problem on the part of our parishes. Much can be done in this field without formal organization. Catholic parishes need to become sensitive to the type of neighborliness that is already to be found in some blocks. This can be stimulated in an informal way without necessarily institutionalizing it. Our parish studies have shown that a majority of the aging and chronically ill are cared for in their own homes or in the homes of relatives.

2. The interest of various Catholic organizations in the aging needs to be stimulated. This is especially the case with respect to the aging and chronically ill in municipal hospitals, nursing homes, and

those receiving Old-Age Assistance and living in boarding houses.

3. In some places we find a beginning of an awareness that the institution for the aging may serve as a center for such persons with a program geared to the level of the neighborhood. This, of course, should not mean a patronizing attitude on the part of the institution. In fact, one of the real dangers to be avoided is the tendency to treat the aging as children.

4. There is great need for more research on problems of the aging. We have made a beginning in our study of the aging in a Cleveland parish, published in 1954. We also collaborated with the Catholic Charities of the Archdiocese of St. Louis in a study entitled *Older People in the Family, the Parish and the Neighborhood,* published in 1955. We have recently initiated a similar study in an area in Buffalo, New York.

5. Catholic Charities can do a good deal toward stimulating interest in its service-training programs for the personnel of institutions for the aging by building up a body of material such as is not available at the present time. This can be done only by research.

6. There is need for a new type of volunteer service in the program of institutions for the aging. Our present institutional staffs are inadequate. The only way to make them more nearly adequate seems to be by a new type of volunteer service, carried on by people who can give a considerable amount of time each week to actual work with the aging in institutions. This calls for systematic planning on the part of the institutions. It is only by such planning between the institutions and Catholic Charities that an effective volunteer program can be worked out.

7. Catholic Charities, of course, will want to cooperate with other organizations, both governmental and voluntary, in working out community approaches to the problems of the aging.

8. Catholic Charities must work with institutions for the aging in planning constructive leisure-time programs within the institutions, based as far as possible on the thinking of their guests. They should be encouraged to work out their own programs to meet their own needs.

9. There is great need in Catholic institutions for the aging for

carefully thought out programs of physical and vocational therapy which would make it possible for the aging who have any strength left to continue to have the feeling that they can do something constructive and that they have an opportunity to do so. This is the best antidote for that depressive mentality which one finds in so many of the institutions for the aging today.

The Beginnings of National Organization

The establishment of the National Conference of Catholic Charities in Washington in 1910 was an important departure in the work of Catholic Charities in the United States. It realized the hopes of the pioneer lay leaders who received their inspiration from association with non-Catholic American organizations, notably the Charity Organization Society of New York. The ideal of these lay leaders, members of the Society of St. Vincent de Paul, could not have been realized in 1910 without the vision of the late Dr. William J. Kerby, then professor of sociology at the Catholic University of America, and Monsignor Thomas J. Shahan, then Rector of Catholic University. They had a broad vision of the place that a national organization, bringing together the various charities of the Church, might have in bridging the gulf between Catholics and the rest of the American community. They felt that this was the only way to give lay leadership its proper stature. They felt also that it would do much toward eliminating the isolation of Catholic organizations, one from another.

One of the immediate objectives of the National Conference was to establish local conferences of Catholic Charities which would bring together the various Catholic organizations in different cities throughout the country. These local conferences really helped to pave the way for the later city-wide and diocesan-wide organizations of Catholic Charities. Another important function of the new National Conference of Catholic Charities, as its founders conceived it, was the development of an independent and trained lay leadership, both volunteer and professional, in Catholic Charities. This objective came about quite naturally because the leadership up to that time had been almost entirely a lay leadership. While there were a few priests active in the work, they had really been inspired by the lay leaders.

Closely allied with the objective of developing trained lay leaders was the establishment of training schools for social workers under Catholic auspices. The first of these schools was set up at Loyola University in Chicago in 1914. Later followed Fordham University School of Social Service, New York, in 1916; St. Louis University School of Social Service, in 1930; Boston College School of Social Work, in 1936; Our Lady of the Lake College, Worden School of Social Service, San Antonio, in 1942. The National Catholic School of Social Service in Washington was established by the National Council of Catholic Women in 1921. The Catholic University School of Social Work was begun in 1934. In 1947, the National Catholic School of Social Service and the Catholic University School of Social Work merged and now operate under the title of National Catholic School of Social Service of the Catholic University.

An important objective that the founders of the National Conference of Catholic Charities cherished from the beginning was the development of a body of literature on Catholic Charities. As a step toward this goal a *Directory of Catholic Charities in the United States* was published by the National Conference in 1920. The founders also took over the *"St. Vincent de Paul Quarterly"* which was published by the St. Vincent de Paul Society from 1895 until it was absorbed by the *"Catholic Charities Review"* in 1916.

In 1931, the National Conference published a volume by the writer entitled, *Catholic Charities in the United States: History and Problems*. A study on *Children's Institutions* by Monsignor John M. Cooper was published in 1931; and in 1948 *Services to Children in Institutions* by Cecelia McGovern, Ph.D. More recently a study entitled *A Study of the Aging in a Cleveland Parish* has been released. The Conference of Religious, which is a special division of the National Conference, has been responsible for three important pieces of literature: *The Catholic Maternity Home; The Housemother—a Member of the Institutional Team* by Sister Mary Charles Keane, R.S.M.: and *Sisters in Social Service*.

Organization of Diocesan Charities

The writer has pointed out in his previously cited *Catholic Charities in the United States: History and Problems:*

After 1900 a number of members of the St. Vincent de Paul Society became dissatisfied with the purely parochial outlook in charity work. As men of affairs, some of them were insistent that business methods should be carried over in their service of the poor.

The members of the St. Vincent de Paul Society had learned their lessons from association with the Charity Organization Society of New York City. Here is their own story:

In caring for the large number of families assigned to us we have been aided in keeping many of them from breaking up by the cooperation of the Charity Organization Society. . . .

As a result of their experience in dealing with other organizations, the St. Vincent de Paul leaders, notably those in New York and Baltimore, came to recognize the importance of a central clearinghouse for all Catholic Charities in the various cities. They felt that the central organization needed qualified and trained personnel. Thus they laid the foundation of our present city-wide organizations of Catholic Charities. We have at the present time 305 of these organizations in 110 Catholic dioceses in the United States.

These organizations from the beginning had one central theme, namely, the coordination, improvement, and development of Catholic Charities. They began with the idea of a clearinghouse to supplement existing organizations. It was assumed, of course, that many parishes could take care of their ordinary problems, but there were many other parishes in which great need existed but which had no organization. Then came the idea of improving the existing organizations. Intake of Catholic children's institutions became an important function of these organizations because very few Catholic institutions had intake service. There was the further need of implementing the work of the institutions, of placing children in boarding and free homes as well as adoptive homes. Heretofore, there had been no systematic adoption service except that provided by the pioneer bureaus set up by the St. Vincent de Paul Society.

It would be very difficult in a brief space to analyze the various services carried on by city-wide organizations of Catholic Charities. A considerable number of these organizations are essentially child-caring organizations that deal with the intake of Catholic children's homes, and place children in free and boarding homes and in adoptive homes. Sometimes they have what might be considered complete diocesan coverage in the field of child care, and sometimes they are limited to the diocesan city. Sometimes they have only one office in the central diocesan city, while in some of the larger places, as in New York and San Francisco, they may have many branches. The extent to which the branches exercise autonomy differs greatly from one diocese to another and sometimes there are variations even within the same diocese.

About two-thirds of the total number of city-wide organizations of Catholic Charities have more or less extensive programs of family service, usually with a considerable volume of relief. In some dioceses the local parish organizations have relief funds, but as a general rule there are some supplementary diocesan funds for Catholic relief. We find these supplementary funds even in cities in which Catholic organizations participate in Community Chests, and also in cities in which there are no Chest funds available for relief.

To the services of city-wide organizations of Catholic Charities there has been added in a number of cities in recent years a central service for the aging, including intake service for institutions for the aging. A number of organizations of Catholic Charities in recent years have been promoting self-studies on the part of child-caring institutions and also homes for the aging.

In a few cities Catholic Charities has been stimulating programs of self-help in various neighborhoods or areas within its jurisdiction. This is one of the developments that offer a bright promise for the future.

In its early days Catholic Charities stressed in each city the great importance of stimulating volunteer lay leadership not only in the various parishes but also throughout the entire city. In recent years there has been an increasing interest in highly specialized services and less emphasis on the stimulation of volunteer service, on both a parish and city-wide basis. In this respect Catholic organizations for the most part have only followed the trend in the general field of American social welfare. It has been pointed out that this trend is due to the type of training received by the executives and workers in the various Catholic as well as other schools of social service.

Some of the leaders in Catholic Charities, however, instead of criticizing the schools of social service, are now re-examining their own thinking and are asking themselves: How much are we contributing to the thinking of schools of social service which would be helpful to them in broadening their programs so that they can halt the drift toward the type of specialization that isolates them from the community and from other disciplines? Others in Catholic Charities see a new danger in this reaction against highly specialized services. They feel there is danger of losing some of the gains which have been made in the type of specialization necessary to deal with certain kinds of problems that Catholic institutions and agencies are facing. While there is a recognition of the need for a broader approach and the development of a program that will come closer to the true mission of the Church in the field of welfare, it is recognized also that there are children and families that present very difficult problems which call for highly specialized services.

Our Holy Father's Christmas Eve address of 1952 opened a new day in the focus and point of view of Catholic Charities throughout the world. His Holiness pointed out:

The great temptation in an age that calls itself social—when, besides the Church, the State, the municipality, and other public bodies devote themselves so much to social problems—is that when the poor man knocks on the door, people, even believers, will just send him away to an agency or social center, to an organization, thinking that their personal obligation has been sufficiently fulfilled by their contributions in taxes or voluntary gifts to those institutions.

Undoubtedly, the poor man will receive your help in that way. But often he counts also on yourselves, at least on your words of kindness and comfort. Your charity ought to resemble God's, Who came in person to bring His help. This is the meaning of the message of Bethlehem. . . .

This original statement has been implemented by many later statements made by our Holy Father. In his message to the St. Louis meeting of the National Conference of Catholic Charities in 1953, His Holiness had this to say:

The realization that the duty of charity binds each and every one of the faithful will also give new impetus to the practice of charity through neighborly service. Charity must never end at home; but it is there that it begins. The importance of the neighborly mutual help which people can organize for themselves, in countries less materially developed, is evident. . . .

The words of our Holy Father in regard to social service or charity as the function of every neighborhood are in line with our traditional teaching concerning the Mystical Body of Christ. In every neighborhood we have the coming together of Christians, and wherever Christians are joined together there is Christ in their midst.

We should not have to return to the early Church to get new inspiration in regard to the practise of Christian neighborly service. We can constantly receive inspiration through the emphasis placed by the Church on Christ's teaching and example. This makes charity and neighborly service a part of the work of every individual Christian. Here is the real basis of the new doctrine in respect to self-help organization about which we hear so much in so many communities throughout the world. It encompasses all the principles that are being applied in the Indian villages and in many eastern and western African communities at the present time.

It is the great hope for the progress of Christianity in the so-called less developed countries throughout the world, and also for the material progress of these countries. It is the great challenge confronting all religious groups in every American community. In the neighborhood and in the block, they can work together on their common problems. They can work together in dealing with the forces making

for disorganization, for the breakdown of family life, for delinquency, for lack of law enforcement, and all the other evils now be-
setting American communities.

This truly Christian approach to the community does not mean
that we are going to abandon our highly specialized services. We
will still utilize these services because they are necessary to meet the
needs of many of God's neglected children.

IV

JEWISH SOCIAL WORK TODAY

BY

ALTER F. LANDESMAN

Executive Director, Hebrew Educational Society

While the commemoration by the Jewish community of the Tercentenary of the first settlement of Jews in New Amsterdam is fresh in our memories, it is fitting to review the development of Jewish social service in this country, and to indicate some recent trends. The first Jewish contingent to settle here consisted of twenty-three Dutch-Brazilian refugees who were so impoverished that they did not have enough to pay their passage money. The New Amsterdam colonists did not want them to remain. Peter Stuyvesant, in a letter to his superiors, the Dutch West India Company, on September 22, 1654, gave as one of his reasons for his objections to their settlement that "the Deaconry [is] also fearing that owing to their present indigence they might become a charge in the coming winter." [1] The Company did not yield to Stuyvesant's petition, and on April 26, 1655, wrote to him:

. . . Therefore, after many deliberations we have finally decided . . . that these people may travel and trade to and in New Netherland, and live and remain there, provided the poor among them shall not become a burden to the company or to the community, but be supported by their own nation. You will now govern yourself accordingly. [2]

It appears that the Jewish newcomers did have to become for a while a charge on the colony, for it was some time before they could

[1] Samuel Oppenheim, *The Early History of the Jews in New York, 1654-1664*, Publication of American Jewish Historical Society, 18, New York, 1909, p. 4.
[2] *Ibid.*, p. 8.

hear from their friends in Holland. The first Jewish merchant and
settler, Jacob Barsimson, who had arrived directly from Holland on
August 22, 1654, only a few weeks before the larger group, was
probably in no financial position, or perhaps was unwilling, to assist
so many of his needy coreligionists.

We learn of the plight of these immigrants from a letter sent on
March 18, 1655, by the minister of the colony, Rev. John Megapolen-
sis to the Classis of Amsterdam. This is what he wrote:

It would have been proper that these had been supported by their own
nation, but they have been at our charge, so that we have had to spend
several hundred guilders for their support. They came several times to
my house, weeping and bewailing their misery, and when I directed them
to the Jewish merchant they said that he would not lend them a single
stiver. Now again in the spring some have come from Holland and report that a great many of that lot would yet follow and then build here
their synagogue. This causes among the congregation here a great deal
of complaint and murmuring. . . . Therefore, we request your Rever-
ences to obtain from the Lords Directors that these godless rascals, who
are of no benefit to the country, but look at everything for their own
profit, may be sent away from here. . . .[3]

The record of Jewish social service during the past three centuries
in this country shows that the problems of immigration and the
adjustment of the newly arrived immigrants to their new environment continued to be one of the major concerns throughout the
period. It also indicates that the Jews not only made every effort to
provide for the care of their indigent and distressed fellow Jews
here and abroad, but that they have taken an active part in
the extraordinary expansion of social welfare activities in America.

The Background of Jewish Social Service

In discussing the structure and program of Jewish social work, it
should be kept in mind that it represents one of the many voluntary
social welfare efforts in the general community. Like the efforts of
other groups, it seeks to relate itself to the common stake which all

[3] *Ibid.*, pp. 52, 73–74.

Americans have in the public welfare program by participating in local and national planning bodies, by affiliating with community chests, and by experimenting and developing new services of value to all. Jewish social workers usually receive their professional training in the general schools of social work.[4]

Besides the characteristics common to all contemporaneous welfare work, Jewish social work aims to meet specifically Jewish needs and has distinctive characteristics. These may be explained by the religious outlook, laws, and traditions of Judaism pertaining to social welfare; by the history and experience of the particular Jewish clientele; and by the special events here and abroad which have affected Jewish life everywhere.

The Jewish Concept of Zedakah

Through the ages, Jewish philanthropy has been known as *zedakah,* the practice of righteousness, and *gemilith hasadim,* bestowing of kindness, the rendering of services which include elements of personal helpfulness. Both of these concepts are deeply imbedded in the legislation, ideals, and standards of the Bible, in Talmudic and rabbinic literature.[5] They have become an integral part of the Jewish way of life, and are spelled out in great detail in the codes of law of Maimonides (1135-1204); Jacob ben Asher (fourteenth century); Joseph Caro (1488-1575); and in the works of the great teachers throughout the ages. Many of the modern Jewish theologians and scholars, including Kaufman Kohler, Solomon Schechter, Jehudah Bergman, and others, have likewise devoted some of their work to Jewish philanthropy. All of these have exercised a profound influence on Jewish benevolent thought and social endeavors.

[4] *Cf.* H. L. Lurie, "The Approach and Philosophy of Jewish Social Welfare," *"Jewish Social Quarterly,"* Vol. XXIX, No. 3, March, 1953; Martin M. Cohn, "Jewish Social Work," *The Social Work Year Book,* 1954, pp. 285 ff.

[5] The transliteration of Hebrew words in this chapter, as in others, is that of the author himself. Jehudah Bergman, *Ha-Zedakah B'Israel,* Jerusalem, 5704 (1944); Ephraim Frisch, *An Historical Survey of Jewish Philanthropy,* Macmillan Company, New York, 1924; Boris Bogen, *Jewish Philanthropy,* Macmillan Company, New York, 1917; Abraham Cronbach, "Philanthropy in Rabbinical Literature and Jewish Philanthropic Institutions in the Middle Ages," in *Religion and its Social Setting,* The Social Press, Cincinnati, 1933, pp. 99-153.

That feeling of sympathy with those in want which moves more or less every human heart, prompting it to helpfulness (writes Kaufman Kohler) has been developed by the genius of the Jew, owing to his patriarchal traditions, into a deep and firm sense of duty, into a law of social righteousness, so that everyone who has should be impressed with the feeling of responsibility for the weal and woe of him who has not.[6]

"It is our bounden duty," writes Maimonides in his *Mishneh Torah,* "to be more scrupulously observant of the precepts relating to Charity (*mizevot zedakah*) than of all positive commandments: for charity is the sign of the just seed of Abraham, our father, of whom it is written: 'for I have known him, to the end that he may command his children to do justice.' . . ."[7] All were expected to contribute to the maintenance of the communal welfare agencies, whether they could give large or small gifts. "It is a duty," writes Jacob ben Asher in the *Tur Yoreh Deah (Hilkot Zedakah,* the Laws of Charity), "to give as much as one can afford. . . . A man should consider that God is near to the cry of the poor and also that God has a covenant with the poor" (Exodus 22:22, 26).

As for the Jew who experienced persecutions, expulsions, wars, and exile, and saw how few of his brethren anywhere were able to retain within the same family great wealth over very long periods of time—Rabbi Jacob bids him consider further

that the revolving wheel of life makes it certain that he himself must eventually come to such a pass (poverty), and if not he, his son or his grandson. And he should not be influenced by the thought, why shall I reduce my possessions by giving to the poor? For he should know that his money is naught but a trust fund to be used in accordance with the will of Him Who entrusted it, and His will is that he distribute thereof to the poor, and that is the best portion He derives from it. . . .[8]

While rabbinic literature emphasizes the high esteem in which the poor are held, and their close relation to God, Judaism never idealized poverty and deprivation. It considered poverty as great suffering

---

[6] Kaufman Kohler, *The Historical Development of Jewish Charity,* Ark Publishing Company, Cincinnati, 1915, p. 8.

[7] Matnot Aniyyim, *Portions of the Poor,* Chapter 10, Par. 1.

[8] *Cf.* Frisch, *op. cit.,* pp. 64–67.

and as a degenerative force to be justified only on the ground that it is a test both to the rich and to the poor; to the rich man whether his wealth will spoil him and harden him against the poor; to the poor man whether his deprivation will embitter him and make him rebellious against the affliction. Loss of independence was regarded as one of the greatest hardships connected with poverty, and, therefore, labor which helps secure one's needs was raised to the level of a religious institution.

Naturally, Judaism frowned upon the mortification of the flesh by dire poverty and never encouraged such a thing as organized poverty. It had no mendicant orders. Judaism's prohibition of celibacy, and the acceptance of the institution of marriage as an obligation of the individual, not only served to counteract any tendency to idealize poverty, but influenced greatly the whole Jewish attitude toward the problem of charity.[9]

Anyone who reads rabbinic literature will realize what stress is laid on the manner in which we do our "charity" (*zedakah*). *Matan b'seter*—giving secretly—became a great principle. "To help the poor by lending him money or otherwise facilitating his mode of support is more meritorious than to give him alms." Of the eight different grades of donors, which Maimonides enumerates in his code, he places in the highest class the one who aids the poor man to support himself by advancing him funds or by helping him to some lucrative occupation; and in the second group, those who give charity without knowing the recipient, and without the recipient knowing the donor.[10]

Above all else, "charity" was not a harsh and narrow conception of duty or righteousness. The concepts of *zedakah* and *gemilith hasadim* were inseparable. We read in the Talmudic tractate of *Sukkah* (49b) the following:

Rabbi Eliezer further stated, the reward of *zedakah* (charity) depends entirely upon the extent of the *hesed* in it (the kindness, grace, gentleness, and sympathy that accompany the act) for it is said, "Sow to yourselves

---

[9] Solomon Schechter, "Jewish Philanthropy," *Studies in Judaism*, Third Series, Jewish Publication Society of America, Philadelphia, 1924, pp. 238 ff., 273–275.
[10] *Mishneh Torah* 1c., par. 7–14.

according to *zedaḳah* (charity) but reap according to the *ḥesed* (kindness)" (Hosea 10:12). Our rabbis taught that in three respects is *gemilith hasadim* superior to *zedaḳah*: *zedaḳah* can involve only one's money but *gemilith hasadim* can involve one's person and one's money, charity is for the poor, the latter for the rich and the poor. *Zedaḳah* can be given to the living only. *Gemilith hasadim* can be done both to the living and to the dead.

It is against this background that Jewish communities organized their network of charity services, whether in London, Amsterdam, Warsaw, or Vilna, which served as models for the Jewish immigrants who settled in America. To feed the hungry, clothe the naked, visit the sick, bury the dead, ransom the captive, educate the fatherless, provide the poor maiden with a dowry enabling her to marry, were some of the elements of personal helpfulness which every Jewish community sought to provide.

Jewish Community Organization

The Jewish community pattern in America differs from that of Jews in all other countries.[11] Unlike most communities in Europe that exercised some sort of authority over Jews, among other things compelling them to be members of a congregation, American Jews have no recognized central organ of self-rule with authority to speak for all Jews as Jews. There is no hierarchical authority to organize them or to direct their affairs. Actually the term "Jewish community" is an abstraction. It has been used as a simple way of expressing the organized interests of those who might be included within the Jewish population.

Judaism makes no ecclesiastical distinction between laity and clergy. The rabbi's authority is personal, in proportion to his reputation for learning and piety. As the term connotes, he is a teacher or master with a special fitness for the interpretation of the Torah and for community leadership. Thus the duties of charity and its administration rest on rabbi and layman alike.

[11] *Cf.* Charles S. Bernheimer, "What is a Jewish Community?" *"Jewish Social Quarterly,"* Vol. XXVIII, No. 3, March, 1952, pp. 219–227.

Instead of a comprehensive community, there have been various associations of individuals around specific and restricted forms of group interest. In some instances the specific activity or interest of a group was so wide in scope that it tended to draw in a large proportion of the Jewish population. Jewish philanthropy because of its broad scope represents the form of group interest which in many American cities has attracted the largest adherence of Jews.

Early Developments

In its first century and a half, the growth of the Jewish community in America was slow; Jewish settlements were small in number, and fairly homogeneous in composition. As late as 1818, the Jewish population was about 3,000 Sephardic Jews, mostly from Holland and England, and Ashkenazic Jews of Central European origin, who had gone to the seaport cities of New York, Newport, Philadelphia, Savannah, Charleston, and adjacent parts.

With the arrival of larger numbers of Jewish immigrants, especially of German Jews, from about 1820 to 1870, and East European Jews, which began a little later, new communities were developed in the west and south, and the population rose to about 15,000 in 1840; to above 50,000 in 1848; and to as many as 230,257 in 1877.[12]

The first institutions to be established by these early settlers were synagogues, and in these early days they not only provided a place for congregational worship and educational programs for the young, but became responsible for all Jewish philanthropic activities. This pattern of social service not only followed Jewish traditional practice, but conformed to the tendencies prevailing at that time in America, when social work was carried on mostly on a private basis and along sectarian lines by the various churches.

The history of the oldest Jewish congregation in this country, Shearith Israel Synagogue in New York, indicates that it distributed

---

[12] Joseph Jacobs, "Jewish Population in the U.S.," *American Jewish Year Book,* American Jewish Committee, New York, 1927, p. 339; *cf.* Louis Finkelstein, ed., *The Jews: Their History, Culture and Religion,* Vol. IV, Jewish Publication Society of America, Philadelphia, 1949, p. 1221.

money to the poor, free seats in the synagogue, *matzoh* before the Passover holidays, wood during the winter, and provided free burial and to some extent free medical aid and loans free of interest. It also established a system of annuities for its members who because of illness, old age, or other reasons, were unable to care for themselves. Every effort was made by the congregation to prevent "a Jew from going to live . . . at the poor house," where he would be denied a Jewish environment and *kosher* food. In 1827, when two Jewish boys were left as orphans in New York City, one was adopted by a Jew in the community and the Shearith Israel and Bnai Jeshurun Congregations paid for the upkeep of the other boy, who was boarded out.[13]

The founders of the first Jewish hospital in this country, called Jews' Hospital, in New York City, and now known as Mount Sinai Hospital, held their meetings in the Portuguese Congregation for three years prior to 1855, when the hospital building on Twenty-eighth Street was opened.[14] When a controversy arose whether postmortem examinations should be permitted in the hospital, a letter was sent to Reverend N. M. Adler, Chief Rabbi of all Jews in the British Empire, asking his advice on the subject, and the records of the Board of the Institution indicated that every effort was made to follow his opinion.[15]

The synagogues not only assisted the poor within their own community, but in times of emergency answered the requests of others, including Jewish and non-Jewish causes both here and abroad. They also contributed for the poor of Palestine, through the various messengers (*meshulahim*) who arrived here to seek such aid from time to time, beginning with Moses Malki in 1759.

When Jewish immigration increased, new organizations were founded to handle the charitable work. But even these organizations were to a greater or less degree affiliated with the various syna-

[13] See Chapter on "Philanthropy" in Hyman B. Grinstein, *The Rise of the Jewish Community of New York, 1654–1860*, Jewish Publication Society of America, Philadelphia, 1945, pp. 131–162 ff.

[14] *Ibid.*

[15] Joseph Hirsh and Beka Doherty, *The First Hundred Years of Mt. Sinai Hospital of New York, 1852–1952*, Random House, New York, 1952, pp. 37–38.

gogues. When a yellow fever epidemic was raging in 1798, Gershon M. Seixas, minister of Shearith Israel, established the *Kalfe Zedekah Matan Beseter,* a charity society whose aim was to distribute its funds secretly, without divulging the names or number of the recipients.

In 1822, the Ashkenazic immigrants established the Hebrew Benevolent Society (*Meshibot Nefesh*), which became an affiliate of the Bnai Jeshurun Synagogue when it was formed in 1825. Various women's organizations, especially characteristic of American Jewish charitable work, developed to cope with the increasing needs; but all of these, too, were attached to synagogues.

During this pioneering period there was no distinction between "religious" and "secular" welfare. But with the influx of tremendous numbers of immigrants, especially between 1881 and 1914, when some 2,000,000 Jews entered the United States from Eastern Europe, the need for more and varied assistance led to the formation of numerous organizations that cut across the line and authority of the synagogue. The various social service functions passed from the synagogue to autonomous separate societies which sprang up by the hundreds to cope with the needs of the growing community.

Since the German Jews were among the older settlers and in a better economic condition than the newly arrived immigrants from Eastern Europe, charitable and social service institutions continued to be principally under their control. Because of differences in religious and cultural outlook, these newly arrived immigrants often clashed with the older settlers. Before long, these East European Jews established their own network of social service agencies, adding to the diversity of social service programs.

Recent Expansion of Social Services

Even a brief examination of Jewish agencies today indicates not only the magnitude of social services provided by the Jewish community but also the tremendous expansion in all areas to meet changing needs. From a small homogeneous group traditionally served by the congregation as the central relief agency, the Jewish community in the United States has grown to approximately 5,000,000, constituting almost one-half of the Jews of the entire world. While seventy-five per cent of American Jews live in the ten largest cities, Jews have been found to reside in every part of this country, in some 5,000 cities, towns, and villages. It is impossible to determine the total giving by Jews to all causes, Jewish and non-Jewish, but, on the basis of reports which the Council of Jewish Federations and Welfare Funds (C.J.F.W.F.) receives regularly from the great majority of Jewish fund-raising organizations, we may estimate the present total contribution to philanthropy by American Jewry through Jewish agencies to be about $200,000,000 a year. A peak was reached in 1948 when $201,405,000 was raised by local central community campaigns alone, $65,841,000 of the total coming from New York City.

The events during and since World War II, the calamitous destruction of a large portion of world Jewry by Nazism, the need to find homes for the displaced and homeless refugees, the establishment of Israel on May 14, 1948, and various local needs have aroused American Jewry to great heights of generosity and responsibility.

Although the amounts raised since the peak year continue to show a declining trend, the federation and welfare funds campaign of 1954, obtained about $107,500,000 or eight per cent less than in 1953.

Seventy-two cities outside of New York in 1954 showed a continuing high degree of participation in the central community-wide drives —twenty-six contributions per hundred Jewish residents in these cities. It should be noted, however, that eighty-nine per cent of the total funds came from seventeen per cent of all givers.

To this sum collected by Jewish welfare funds, should be added the funds received from other sources. The income was quite substantial, even if the over-all total cannot be determined. Some sixty-five national, domestic, and overseas agencies recorded a total income of about $35,100,000 in 1954, which they received from their own independent campaigns and other sources. Nor are estimates available of the substantial funds raised by Jewish religious and secular institutions, both local and national, which are not related to central financing.

Besides all these funds are the sums raised in capital funds campaigns for the construction or improvement of institutional facilities, the funds privately transmitted abroad over and above the central fund-raising agencies, and the Jewish gifts to non-sectarian causes.

Comparison of the contributions noted in the foregoing paragraphs with the yearly expenses of organized Jewish charity in New York City in 1728, estimated at about $150, and in 1859 at about $18,000, or even with the estimated $34,000,000 in 1923 for all of the United States, helps us appreciate the significance of present-day Jewish giving.[16]

Overseas and Immigration Services

When we examine the budget of the American Jewish community we find that every type of social service is offered by a variety of organizations. On the basis of their field of operation these social service agencies may be divided into two groups: one concerned with overseas and immigration services, and with assistance to Israel; and the other comprising the local and national social agencies.

During the past few years overseas needs have received major attention, absorbing much of the energy and manpower available for communal service.[17] The United Jewish Appeal (U.J.A.), the major agency in this country that concerns itself with these needs, paid in 1955 $54,865,578 to its main beneficiaries; $930,280 went to the United Service for New Americans (U.S.N.A.), which in August, 1954, merged with H.I.A.S., forming United Hias Service; and to the New York Association for New Americans (N.Y.A.N.A.). (These items were smaller than in previous years due to the drop in immigration of Displaced Persons into the United States. Only 1,800 Jews came to the United States in 1955, compared with 5,500 in 1954; 16,973 in 1951; 37,482 in 1949; 16,000 in

---

[16] See Morris D. Waldman, *Nor by Power,* International Universities Press, Inc., New York, 1953, Part III, "Pioneering and Progressing in Philanthropy," pp. 297 ff.

[17] S. A. Goldsmith, "Jewish Philanthropy—1923," *"American Hebrew,"* Vol. 114, No. 4, December 7, 1923, pp. 108 ff.; Julius Drechsler, "The Trend of Jewish Communal Life in the United States," *"Jewish Social Service Quarterly,"* Vol. I, No. 3, November, 1924, p. 12; Grinstein, *op. cit.,* p. 161.

1948, and 25,000 in 1947.) An allocation of $17,369,202 was made to the American Jewish Joint Distribution Committee (J.D.C.), which concerns itself with a wide range of relief, educational, religious, and vocational services in twenty-five lands. With these and other funds the J.D.C. spent over $25,000,000 for its many services in 1955. It conducted the Malben program, the second largest medical program in Israel, which in 1955 gave medicine and help to some 18,500 men, women, and children, providing 6,800 beds for the care of the aged, tubercular, and sufferers from chronic diseases; and assisting religious schools, destitute scholars, and refugee rabbis. It appropriated some $8,000,000 to meet the needs of various European communities, and financed urgently needed programs of feeding, medicine, and education, in Morocco and other Moslem lands. A total of $36,566,096 went to the United Israel Appeal that devotes its funds to the development of Israel through financing of programs for immigration, relief, and housing for immigrants, agricultural settlements, and other services.

Besides the United Jewish Appeal there were a number of other agencies raising funds for overseas aid, especially for Israel, reporting an income of $18,300,000 in 1954. These included Hadassah with a budget of some $8,500,000 for its medical and child-care program in Israel; the United Hias Service that spent $2,340,000 for the year ending August, 1955; the National Committee for Labor Israel and the Pioneer Women's Organization; the American Fund for Israel Institutions, and a number of other smaller and distinct efforts.

Local Social Services

The group of agencies that serve local and national needs offer a wide range of services varying from community to community. A study made by the Council of Jewish Federations in seventy-nine communities (outside New York City) showed that they allocated for local services some $22,438,000 in 1954, an increase of about 100 per cent since 1946. The majority participated in non-sectarian community chests for all or some part of their financial needs. In this entire group, hospitals and other health services accounted for 30.3

per cent of the total expenditures in 1954; community centers and related services for 24.3 per cent; family, care for the aged, and child services 27.7 per cent; and Jewish education twelve per cent. In smaller communities with a Jewish population of under 15,000, the largest portion of all local expenditures went for community centers and Jewish education. Sixty per cent of the total income of local health and welfare agencies came from payments for service; eight per cent from public tax funds; eight per cent from contributions; and three per cent from investments and miscellaneous sources. In New York City, the Federation of Jewish Philanthropies allotted $13,029,445 for the period July 1, 1955, to June 30, 1956, of which 38.09 per cent went for medical care; 15.32 per cent for family welfare and vocational; 16.01 per cent for child care; 14.05 per cent for community centers; 4.88 per cent for religious education; 3.87 per cent for the aged; and 2.29 per cent for camps.

Fields of Service

1. Medical Care

Of sixty-one hospitals reporting to the C.J.F.W.F. forty-one are general hospitals; twenty special hospitals including national and local tuberculosis, chronic disease, psychiatric, and other special services. In 1954, they treated 491,779 patients, with the daily census on January 1 showing 10,834 in the general hospitals, and 3,085 in the special hospitals. Fewer than half of the patients—about forty-four per cent—were Jewish.

The Jewish Federations are spending more and more of their money in this field of medical care; for example, it amounts currently to 38.09 per cent of the total budget of the New York Federation of Jewish Philanthropies. Some of the hospitals were constructed for the primary purpose of caring for the Jewish sick by providing a Jewish environment and *kosher* food, in addition to providing facilities for Jewish physicians. The majority, however, are motivated by the desire to contribute their share to the medical care of the entire population.

In a number of communities where Jewish hospitals were being constructed, as in the case of the Long Island Jewish Hospital, or where there were already established hospitals that did not provide *kosher* food, there has been an active movement on the part of important elements in the Jewish population to require these hospitals to provide their Jewish patients with *kosher* food.

2. *Family Service*

During 1954, nearly 49,000 families received counseling, financial assistance, and other services from Jewish family agencies. Since the establishment of public relief on a wide scale, the Jewish family agency has changed from a relief agency to a social service agency offering programs of family welfare, counseling aid to refugees and immigrants, Passover assistance, and other services. Only a small percentage of the clientele (mostly recent immigrants) of these agencies received financial assistance. As for the rest of the clients, the predominant caseloads of many agencies included people with emotional problems. Some of them did not manifest any monetary need and even paid part or all of the cost of the counseling services.

3. *Child Care*

There has been a steady decline in this area of service due to the fact that government aid to dependent children has made it possible for children to be maintained in family homes. Three-fourths of the child-care institutions operating under Jewish auspices in 1933 have been closed, placement and shelter care being shifted from institutions to specialized treatment in family homes, foster homes, and specialized smaller institutions.

Of the 3,978 children under direct supervision by fifty-two child-care agencies on December 31, 1954, 31.7 per cent, or 1,234, were in institutions; some 46.4 per cent, or 1,823, in foster homes; 19.6 per cent, or 858, with parents; and all of the others in homes of other relatives. While the population of children's institutions has decreased, the need for child guidance and psychiatric services is increasing greatly, and agencies such as the Jewish Board of Guardians and its group of agencies in New York City are faced with long waiting lists.

4. *The Aged*

The rapidly increasing number of aged persons in the population requires additional provision of facilities and services to meet the residential, physical, psychological, and recreational needs of these older persons. Seventy-one homes cared for more than 9,000 residents in 1954, many of them modifying their institutional programs, expanding their medical and other services, and a number constructing new facilities or remodeling old facilities, especially for the chronically ill and the aged.

With government assistance and the various new developments, such as the apartment house projects or residence clubs for the aged, and the special residences provided in city housing projects, many of the older adults prefer to remain in their own homes, going for their recreation to the various community centers which have organized special programs for them, and to the case-work and other agencies with their other problems.

5. *The Jewish Center Movement*

The Jewish community in 1954 celebrated the hundredth anniversary of the founding of the first Young Men's Hebrew Association in Baltimore in 1854, the forerunner of the modern Jewish Community Center. In 1956, the National Jewish Welfare Board, the national coordinating service agency for these organizations, with 348 constituent societies, reported a membership of 565,000 and a professional staff of 1,350 workers; they owned 260 buildings valued at $75,000,000 and had annual operating budgets totaling $16,300,000. From its origin in young people's social or literary societies or in agencies accelerating the Americanization of recently arrived Jewish immigrants, the Center developed in many cities into an all embracing community-serving agency providing a program of social, recreational, educational, cultural, and religious activities, designed to meet the diversified needs of all members of the Jewish family.

In its present form, the Center is a distinctly American contribution to Jewish communal life, striving to perpetuate and develop Jewish life, properly integrated in the life of the general American community.[18]

6. *Jewish Education*

The Jewish religious education of Jewish youth, especially of the poor, has always been accepted as a Jewish communal responsibility. The annual cost of the Jewish school system in the United States is currently (1956) estimated at $38,000,000, most of which comes from parents, individual donors, and congregational sources. Of this, a considerable sum is contributed by Federations of Welfare Funds, and other central fund-raising agencies.[19]

7. *Other Services*

There are numerous other agencies performing important functions, as the mention of some will indicate:

Employment and Vocational Guidance and Services

Organizations for the prevention of delinquency (including such agencies as the Jewish Board of Guardians of New York City and its group of other agencies; Jewish Big Brothers and Sisters; and others)

Hebrew Free Loan Societies (*Gemilith Hasadim*)

Summer camps

Homeless and Unattached (*Hahnosath Orhim*)

National Desertion Bureau

The Free Synagogue Child Adoption Committee

Lakeview Home (a shelter for unmarried mothers)

Hebrew Day Nurseries

Services for Hebrew deaf, blind, and other handicapped persons

Jewish Agricultural Society

Soldiers and Sailors Welfare

Civic Protective Agencies: Community Relations

[18] Current service statistics may be found in the *American Jewish Year Book,* and in the *Yearbook of Jewish Social Service* published by the Council of Jewish Federations and Welfare Funds.

[19] Israel S. Chipkin, "Jewish Education in the United States at the Mid-Century," "*Religious Education,*" Vol. XLVIII, No. 5, September–October, 1953, pp. 327–350.

Educational, Cultural, and Research
Chaplaincy Services: Military and Veteran Services.

Some Trends and New Developments in Jewish Social Work[20]

1. *Increased Coordination through Central Planning and Financing of Philanthropic Work*

Despite the great number of creedal, social, and ideological differences that still persists, the Jewish community has sufficiently matured to accept more and more the concept that there are matters of interest which require common support by all. Federations of Jewish Philanthropies, or central fund-raising organizations bearing various names, are now to be found in every community with five or more communal agencies. Organized at first in 1896 (one of the Jewish contributions to American social work) in Boston and Cincinnati, these federations and welfare funds, under the impact of recent events here and abroad, have extended their functions beyond those of mere fund collection into other areas of community interest, and into central planning.

Through the Council of Jewish Federations and Welfare Funds, with which several hundred communities are affiliated, and the National Conference of Jewish Communal Service, the Jewish layman and the professional have opportunity to discuss problems of community organization, financing, local-national relations, overseas needs and programs, and other problems pertaining to Jewish social welfare. Although organized merely as a conference group with an annual meeting, the C.J.F.W.F and N.C.J.C.S. exercise throughout the year an important influence in Jewish social welfare.[21]

[20] Louis Kraft, *A Century of the Jewish Community Center Movement,* The National Jewish Welfare Board, Jewish Community Center Centennial Committee, New York, 1953; Oscar I. Janowsky, *The Jewish Welfare Board Survey,* Dial Press, New York, 1948, pp. 490 ff.

[21] The reader will find the current trends in Jewish social work reflected on the pages of the issues of the *"Jewish Social Service Quarterly,"* published by the National Conference of Jewish Communal Service. See Fiftieth Anniversary Proceedings,

2. *Extension of Social Services to the Entire Community*

There is a trend toward gearing the Jewish social service program to meet the needs of the entire Jewish community rather than to limit it as in the past to the groups of low economic income. A large proportion of the Jewish population at the present time are American-born, and are situated economically better than their immigrant parents or grandparents. Many today are leaving the congested neighborhoods of the large cities for the suburbs. Some of the services sought by this group are no different, however, from those furnished their parents. They seek marital counseling, child guidance, psychiatric, recreational, and health services, and are willing to contribute toward their cost.

The principle of making social services available to the entire community is now, therefore, being accepted, and with it goes also the understanding that all who can are expected to share the costs. Many agencies have adopted the use of sliding-fee scales for their services.

The Distribution Committee of the Federation of Jewish Philanthropies, in its report for the 1953–1954 budget year, states:

. . . The Committee has tried to have the agencies understand that if the services they render are good, they ought to be available to anyone in the community, not only to the economically necessitous. The disturbed child of a wealthy family is just as much entitled to our understanding and help as is the child of the poor. Indeed, there are undoubtedly instances in which children of the rich need our services much more than some children of the poor. . . . The Committee has made it clear that this in no way is motivated by economy but is solely motivated by the desire to extend the available service to all who need it, whether they can pay for it or not; and to make available to those who can pay for services under appropriate supervision that which cannot be attained in comparable

"Jewish Social Service Quarterly," Vol. XXVI, No. I, September, 1949. Since the delivery of this paper a fully annotated and extensive article on "Jewish Social Work in the United States (1654–1954)" has been published by Herman D. Stein in the 1956 *American Jewish Year Book.* The reader will also find interesting Maurice J. Hexter, "The Next Twenty-five Years in Jewish Communal Service," *"Jewish Social Service Quarterly,"* Vol. XXXII, Fall, 1955.

quality elsewhere; and above all it is not intended to deprive a person who cannot pay for any service. It is further the firm intention of the Distribution Committee that those who need our services and get them should, to the extent that they are able, pay for those services. Such pay ment has, in our view, definite therapeutic value.

3. *Development of a New Leadership*

While the leadership of Jewish philanthropy is predominantly under the control of the big givers and the professionally successful, the composition and control are changing—to the extent that new groups of individuals are constantly reaching the economic level which inspires their interest and participation. The huge and numerous compelling philanthropic appeals of recent years have enlisted the widest participation. Jewish labor leaders with large followings who have in the past kept aloof are now beginning to interest themselves in the philanthropic drives. In a number of communities, the organization of community councils, voluntary associations of selected representatives of all of the important Jewish adult organizations, has improved Jewish relationships among the various groups, and has served as a training ground for new leadership.

4. *Professionalization of Jewish Social Work*

When the volume of social work increased tremendously at the beginning of the century, the work could no longer be done by volunteers. Workers had to be engaged on a full or a part-time basis. Many of these early pioneers of Jewish social service, including rabbis, Jewish intellectuals, and others, while they loved their work and understood their people, lacked training in the social sciences. The demand for a professional training to meet the particular needs of their clients became evident, and a school for Jewish Communal Work was organized in 1917 which, however, lasted only one year. Its successor, the Graduate School for Jewish Social Work, organized in 1925, operated until 1941.

While the growth of professional skills among practitioners is one of the significant developments, since the vast majority of Jewish social workers today are graduates of schools of social work, it is the opinion of many in the field that the need by all branches of Jewish social service of a Jewish education on a high academic level, and of courses that will point out the relevance of Jewish cultural values to the specific requirements of their Jewish clientele, has not diminished. At the present time whatever provision is made by agencies and cultural institutions for in-practice training, and for courses in Jewish social services, does not begin to meet the need.

5. *"Secularization" of Social Services*

Until the middle of the past century, the synagogue was not only the inspiration of all social and philanthropic activities but its chief dispenser. With the impact of modern science and specialization in various fields of endeavor, and the growth of secularism, the synagogue has become separated from social agencies. Rabbis have been active in the development of modern social work, and some even have headed important social agencies. In the case of the Free Synagogue of New York City, founded by Rabbi Stephen S. Wise, a social service department under the leadership of one of its rabbis, Sidney E. Goldstein, was maintained all these years. Nevertheless, Jewish communal agencies are today essentially secular institutions, performing highly specialized functions, maintained by boards of laymen and staffed by professional social workers. The modern rabbi is thought of as only one among professional Jewish workers, and the modern synagogue as one of the independent self-governing institutions in the community, performing a specific task of meeting the religious, educational, and social needs of its members.[22]

At the same time it should be said that in recent years, in the conferences and in the literature of Jewish social work, a great interest has been manifested in defining the nature of Jewish social work and its rationale. Lay leaders, too, are becoming Jewishly more literate and are contributing their share to developing goals for the Jewish community.

[22] Robert L. Katz, "Aspects of Pastoral Psychology and the Rabbinate," *"Jewish Social Service Quarterly,"* Vol. XXIX, No. 4, Summer, 1953, pp. 367–373.

6. *The Impact of Public Welfare Programs and Community Chests on Jewish Social Work*

With the increase in various relief, health, social, and recreational services by public agencies, the validity of certain social services of a distinctively Jewish character is being questioned. There are many who feel that the Jewish communal budget must be re-evaluated, and become constructively concerned with the well-being of the normal population. The scope of Jewish communal activities must be extended to include more of the religious, educational, and cultural agencies.

The development of Community Chests has also complicated the problem of Jewish community organization. Some communities have a "double-barreled" Federation, including, on the one hand, a group of activities financed by the Community Fund, and, on the other, a group of activities outside the Community Fund, the sole responsibility of the Federation. In many cases, the funds available from the Chests have been insufficient to meet the expanding programs, with the result that the call on the Jewish welfare funds for supplementary allotments has been growing from year to year.

7. *Increase in Chaplaincy and Pastoral Services*

Religious teachers or rabbis have never ignored their duties as counselors to individuals. This service has received particular emphasis in the Hasidic movement where the personality of the Rabbi or *Tzadik* has played so important a role. But rabbis generally, as the term connotes, interpreted their function to be primarily that of teachers or interpreters of the Torah, as ministers to the needs of the entire community or congregation, rather than as counselors to individuals. This explains the comparative absence of interest on the part of rabbis in the field of pastoral psychology.[23] It is only in recent years that an increased interest has been manifest. This is especially due to the increased chaplaincy services in the army, navy, and air forces, and to the efforts of the New York Board of Rabbis.

[23] *Cf. ibid.*

The latter group succeeded in placing seventy-four Jewish chaplains in some 150 institutions in Greater New York, and conducts annually a series of seminars and institutes in pastoral psychology and kindred subjects.

V

SPIRITUAL FACTORS IN SOCIAL WORK

BY

LEONARD W. MAYO

Director, Association for the Aid of Crippled Children,
New York City,
and
Chairman, Department of Social Welfare,
Division of Christian Life and Work,
National Council of Churches of Christ
in the United States of America

This subject—"Spiritual Factors in Social Work"—is both intriguing and puzzling. It is intriguing because it sets one thinking of the spiritual foundations of social work, and puzzling because as a result of such contemplation one cannot help wondering whether social workers have failed to convey to others the central purpose of their profession. What I propose to do in this paper, therefore, is to expound modern social work as I see it; to trace its early beginnings briefly, and set forth its motivation and philosophy as I understand them. Those who read these words must then determine for themselves whether there are spiritual factors in social work and, if so, how well they are expressed in practise.

It was once said of a certain history professor that whenever he started any address this side of Homer it was that much sheer gain. I do not propose to start back of Homer or even with him, but I will remind you that the motivation for modern social work has its roots in some of the oldest and hence fundamental yearnings of mankind.

The philosophy of "good works" was an accepted and honored part of the Greek concept of virtue, *i.e.,* consistency between one's acts and his convictions. It was just as clearly a part of the Roman concept of morality, a life lived in accordance with the mores of the times. In both cultures good deeds were given a high place in civic and religious life. To be sure, there is considerable indication that some men engaged in charity in order to improve their prestige in the community and to insure for themselves richer rewards in the hereafter. There is evidence, however, that this unlovely trait in human nature is not confined to ancient man. But surely it was true then, as it is today, that man's humanity to man was not always motivated by the hope or expectation of tangible reward.

One of the earliest writings of ancient times on the subject of charity sets forth various "grades" or levels of giving, starting with purely selfish motives and moving up to a concept as advanced as that which underlies our modern Community Chest movement. The ultimate in giving was described as a situation in which the donor and the recipient do not actually meet and in which the donor must therefore content himself with the mere knowledge that he has done his duty well.

The history of charity and the record of modern times make it clear that all professions that deal directly with people and their social relations have their roots in two fundamental needs of man, the need to love and the need to be loved. The need to love has motivated man to extend his concern and affection beyond himself and frequently to become unselfish in his acts. The need to be loved, which is in part the need of recognition, is equally strong and is akin to the need for food and shelter. Man must have assurance of his spiritual, as well as his physical identity; and thus he constantly strives to establish his relationship to others, to the universe, and to God. As knowledge of the universe expands, it becomes increasingly important for him to feel that he is important and has a place in it. "What is man that Thou art mindful of him?" The history of a nation, a culture, or an individual may be written around the historic and contemporary struggle of man to satisfy these inner needs.

Social work has emerged as a way of helping modern man to achieve these ends in ways that are socially useful and personally rewarding. The history of social work cannot be traced as definitely as that of the ministry, education, medicine, or other professions. In a sense it is an amalgamation of these and perhaps other professions. It is so closely related to our development as a nation that one cannot properly separate the history of social work from our cultural and industrial development. From its beginnings more than a half century ago social work helped to give expression to our early convictions concerning the dignity of man and his inherent needs as a spiritual entity in a free world.

Social work grew out of and still draws upon much that is inherent in the ministry and the church, teaching and the schools, medicine and hospital care, the law and the courts. In turn, and as a result of its convictions and experience in the past half century, it has added something to each of these professions, and to social institutions, in the art of human relations. Each of these professions has developed certain interests and even programs over the years for the benefit of families, children, young people, and the aged. As such programs have moved into the "welfare" area, or have taken on aspects requiring expert knowledge in human relations, the experience and knowledge of social work are frequently required. Lawyers, physicians, and teachers frequently realize that they are confronted with marital problems or problems of parent-child relationships which they are not equipped to handle alone. Increasingly there is an awareness among clergymen that in dealing with emotional, social, and economic problems, they require community facilities not available under church auspices, and skills and experience which they had no opportunity to acquire in seminary training.

It is also generally recognized among professional groups that adequate treatment of many social problems requires basic changes in the community that no one profession or social institution can effect. Note, for example, the problem presented by the city slums which produce fifty-five per cent of all adults who commit crimes, forty-five per cent of all children who get to a juvenile court, and sixty per cent of all those who contract tuberculosis. The eradication of slums is a long, slow, and complicated process which calls for the mobilization of many community groups and forces and a considerable amount of expert technical knowledge in both housing and community leadership.

This is an example of the type of problem to which organized social work has been giving its attention for the past quarter of a century. It not only has many of the skills needful for a community movement of this kind but it possesses the one that is fundamental to action, *i.e.,* the "know how" required to *mobilize* the skills and contributions of many diverse groups and organize them for a central attack on a basic problem.

Social work was just emerging at the turn of the century when the industrial development of the country was accelerating and families who had been living in small towns and in rural areas moved in great numbers into the manufacturing centers. Here the kind ministrations of a friendly neighbor were not always available to individuals in time of trouble and were wholly inadequate to meet mass problems. A feeble-minded or otherwise handicapped child who had been no problem in a rural area, was quite apt to fall into difficulty under the competition and pressures of city life.

As cities mushroomed and social problems multiplied, the need for organization and coordination of effort became apparent. It was not until a quarter of a century later, however, that we began to consider prevention seriously; *i.e.,* to tackle causes as well as to treat symptoms. It is true that papers presented in New York City fifty years ago stressed the importance of preventing poverty, which was then regarded as the root of all social problems. It was not until some years later, however, that we saw the necessity for including other preventive measures, such as those aimed at internal as well as external or environmental causes.

In the middle Eighties the first family agencies devoted to the alleviation of economic and social conditions affecting the family were founded, and at almost the same time social settlements came into being. The former followed the general pattern of the English "charity societies"; the latter, the philosophy of Toynbee Hall.

During this period the professional literature carried such names as Mary Richmond in social case-work, Jane Addams in the settlement field, Florence Kelley in industrial reform, Edward T. Devine in administration and social work education, and Homer Folks in child-welfare and social legislation.

It has been said that "a profession that does not start with the individual does not start, and that a profession that stops with the individual, stops." Actually, social work started with a deep concern for the individual and an equal interest in his total social setting. It was logical then, as this new profession grew and graduate education became a requisite for its practice, that it should reach out to education, mental hygiene, medicine, and psychiatry, and to the findings of sociology and psychology as they became available.

As a result, the history of social work from 1915 to the present time reveals three closely related and almost consecutive developments. The first is the emphasis on organized and disciplined efforts to help the individual in his personal adjustment to his environment, *i.e.,* the process of *social case-work*.

In essence, case-work is a way of helping an individual to achieve a satisfactory adjustment through a series of adaptations between himself and his associates. It is based on the individual's growing understanding of himself and confidence in the social worker who is giving him guidance. The latter must invoke all the resources and relationships of the person being helped, and frequently all the available and appropriate resources of the community. The heart of the process is the interaction between the worker and the individual in which the former must be permissive, enabling, and non-judgmental. The ultimate purpose is to help the person in trouble to gain new insight and motivation and thus move forward toward the solution of his own problem.

The relationship between the social worker and the person seeking help is essentially a spiritual one, aided and cultivated by the skillful use of the "interview" through which every attempt is made to encourage the individual to express, define, and analyze his own problem and to suggest a solution without fear of reprisal, accusation, or even moralization. There is a clear historical and psychological relationship here to the confessional. When adequately conducted, the interview helps to create between the individual seeking help and the social worker a partnership that becomes a dynamic force in the solution of the problems being revealed. Unless he is patently unable to do so, the "client" is encouraged to become and remain the manager of his own affairs, while the role of the social worker is that of an informed and knowledgeable listener and, when indicated, an "organizer" in helping the individual to obtain tangible aid.

The second development is that this awakening interest in the science of human behavior, and in the individual as a functioning member of a family and of other social groups, helped to bring to the fore the concept of social group work. The group-work concept emerged from an analysis of the nature, composition, mechanisms, and operation of all manner of groups in which individuals live and work and play. Thus group work developed as a necessary complement to the individual or case-work approach. In any concept of the individual or the group, each is incomplete without the other. When it comes to modifying the behavior of children or young people, for example, certain individual behavior patterns cannot be changed without some accompanying change on the part of the social group of which the individual is a part.

The nature of groups, the ways in which they influence personality development, the methods of group leadership, and the like have been the subject of intensive study for more than twenty-five years. Settlements, clubs, camps, and church groups of almost every type have come under scrutiny and analysis. Out of this have come new light on human behavior and a substantial enrichment of social-work philosophy. We have long recognized the phenomenon of individual behavior, but not until social workers and social scientists turned their attention to the study of groups did the concept of *group* behavior take shape.

Modern group work consists of the use of the group not only as a vehicle of normal personality development, but as a means of treating the maladjusted and emotionally ill. Hospitals, psychiatric institutions, and some settlements are now conducting treatment groups under expert leadership, many of which are showing substantial results under "group therapy." As an example, children may be given an opportunity to "act out" their hostilities and other deeply set problems through dramatics and the use of puppets or clay-modeling. Thus many problems locked tightly within are brought out in the open where they may be faced and dealt with.

Consideration for the individual, followed by a widening interest in the group, led to the third logical step in the development of social work—namely, concern for the community in which individuals and groups live and for its more effective organization. The third prong of the profession then is community work, or, as it is more familiarly known, *"community organization,"* the word "organization" being used, so to speak, as a verb rather than as a noun. Community organization in social work has to do with the democratic selection of such socially desirable objectives or goals as the construction of a new hospital or playground, the establishment of a new agency, the development of new services for children, the aged, or the handicapped. It is carried on via the process of clarifying the objectives sought and making them clear to the community, organizing the various groups in the community which are essential to the realization of the objectives, analyzing and helping to reconcile differences of opinion and oppositions, and strengthening all indigenous leadership available.

Here then we have a triad—the individual, the group, and the community, with their interacting influences on each other and each with its own distinctive and characteristic behavior.

Several events of the past forty years have done much to shape the content and determine the present status of social work. The first of these perhaps was World War I. It has been said that the war advanced American medicine by at least a full decade. It would be difficult to say whether the same was true of social work, but it is well known that there was a decided upsurge in the organization of new services after the war *because of* the need brought to the fore during that period of crisis.

Another event was the appearance of the mental hygiene movement of the middle Twenties, which threw new light on behavior and personality development.

It was during the great Depression that social work won its spurs as a young profession and learned to apply its new methods and techniques to the alleviation of mass suffering. Though there were some who could not readily make the shift from their recently developed scholarly concepts to the realities of economic disaster, most social workers met the challenge with imagination and vigor.

The advent of the national social security program, the subsequent strengthening of State departments of public welfare, and the increased respect for social work under public auspices combined to create another development of note in social work history.

Then came World War II when, for the first time, a classification number was assigned to social workers along with physicians and nurses, thus giving social work the opportunity to make a contribution as a profession in that period of crisis. The practise of social work under social-work auspices was another significant milestone. When medicine was first practised in industry, and law in business, these steps were regarded as solid gains in recognition of the universal value of medicine and law. The acceptance of social work in new settings gave voice to a basic principle of profound importance: *i.e.,* that what social work has to offer is not exclusively for the poor or the so-called under-privileged, but, as in the instance of medicine, education, and law, it is for all who need it and can use it.

During these forty years social work has been progressing from a cause to a function. For some time after the turn of the century there was a dearth of solid programs and organized and disciplined effort in social work. This was the subject of an address in 1929 by Porter R. Lee, Director of the New York School of Social Work, and then also President of the National Conference of Social Work. Mr. Lee held that while we must never lose the sense of mission inherent in the cause, it must be recognized that causes must be translated into functions and specific programs if basic changes are to be effected. "Banners and parades for the cause," he said, "but a manual of work and discipline for the function."

Social work sustains a relationship to other professions which is perhaps unique. It has no lien on the purposes, the methods, and the philosophy here described. What is unusual about it is that its members have been taught to view each human being as a whole, to call upon the contributions of many other professions and disciplines and every possible resource in the community, and to mobilize them for the benefit of the individual, the group, or the community. This basic tenet at once helps to establish the universality of social work as a profession, as well as its unique relationship to other professions and its dependence on them

I now return to the title of this paper, "The Spiritual Factors in Social Work." As the individual is essentially a spiritual being, and as social work is concerned with the individual in all relationships and with his fulfilment, it is actually dealing with spiritual matters. If its practitioners fail to reveal this in the performance of their professional duties or to reflect it in their personal philosophy, they are falling short of their potentialities and even of their obligations. One may deal with spiritual matters without a full sense of spiritual values, but that does not negate the fact that the subject-matter itself is spiritual.

The key question, therefore, is not "what are the spiritual factors in social work?"—but "is modern social work fulfiling its central purpose?" That is a question which must be answered not only by social workers but by those who are outside the profession and who are thus in a position to observe the performance of its members objectively. I believe that in the past decade there has been a growing appreciation on the part of social workers that ours is essentially a spiritual profession, that we must act in accordance with that concept, and that our methods and programs are means to the end that man may be helped to rediscover himself as a spiritual being with not only a place, but a purpose, in the universe.

VI

THE CHURCHES AND THE NON-SECTARIAN AGENCIES

BY

STANLEY P. DAVIES, Ph.D.

General Director, Community Service Society of New York

At Balliol College, Oxford, England, a memorial tablet is inscribed to Sir Charles Stewart Loch, "once a commoner of this College, for thirty-nine years secretary of the Charity Organization Society" of London, "and all his life a servant and interpreter of charity, unquenchable in spirit and in hope. . . . 1849–1923."

In a foreword to Sir Charles Loch's book, *Three Thousand Years of Social Service,* Charles Mallet wrote: "It was in 1875 that Charles Loch, a young Oxford man of twenty-six . . . set out on the adventure of his life. *It was to draw together from all churches and classes a great society of men and women who might find a common bond and common purpose in the religion of charity fully understood."* [1] Here, happily phrased, is my theme.

Sir Charles himself, in the book to which I have just referred, wrote:

It is assumed that the charity of the religious life, if rightly understood, cannot be inconsistent with that of the social life. . . . The analogies underlying such phrases as "God the Father," "children of God," "brethren," have played a great part in the development of charitable thought in pre-Christian as well as in Christian days. . . . Thus in the word "charity" religious and social associations meet; and thus regarded the word means

[1] Sir Charles Loch, *Three Thousand Years of Social Service,* Charity Organization Society, London, 1938 (reprint).

81

a disciplined and habitual mood in which the mind is considerate of the welfare of others, individually and generally, and devises what is for their real good. . . . Charity thus has no necessary relation to relief or alms. . . . If the world were so poor that no one could make a gift, or so wealthy that no one needed it, charity—the charity of life and of deeds—would remain.

Reaffirming these words of a great and devout precursor in our field, let it be said that "non-sectarian," as applied to the social agency I represent and many similar agencies, despite the negative in its wording, stands for a dynamic concept very positive in meaning and in fact. It neither expresses nor implies negativism toward religion. Quite the contrary! It freely recognizes in religion the greatest well-spring of all that is best in human behavior.

"Non-sectarian" indeed is an unfortunate word to represent that great movement for which it stands. The words "all-sectarian" and "interfaith" more closely reflect the true motivation of these great agencies whose purpose is to serve humanity irrespective of race, creed, color, or national origin. How in keeping with the American tradition it is that agencies so broadly serving should have been formed in the early days of this Republic and should have grown and strengthened as part and parcel of its democratic ideals and practise!

> Give me your tired, your poor,
> Your huddled masses yearning to breathe free,
> The wretched refuse of your teeming shore.
> Send these, the homeless, tempest-tost to me.
> I lift my lamp beside the golden door!

Yes, quoting this verse of Emma Lazarus inscribed within the entrance of the pedestal, the Statue of Liberty beckoned to all the tired, the poor, the politically and economically oppressed of other lands. They came by the hundreds of thousands in the early nineteenth century, 160,000 of them in the year 1848 alone. And, entering through the Port of New York, this is where large numbers of them stayed. Once inside that golden door of America, they crowded into the fearful old-law tenements near the docks. New York and other seaboard cities soon came to have their own "huddled masses," crowded together under unspeakable conditions, still "yearning to breathe free." For many, through many bitter years, the gold they had sought turned out to be dross.

So appalling were the stark needs of these newcomers that alms-giving as a religious duty sprang up on a wide scale. The well-known story of indiscriminate, over-lapping, ill-advised relief began, encouraging chronic pauperism rather than self-help. Begging came to be a profession, and children were trained to be its chief practitioners. The churches and many relief organizations confined their benefactions largely to those of their own religious persuasion or national origin. And they failed to view the problem of distress as a whole and to see what fundamentally and constructively needed to be done about it.

In the winter of 1842–1843 "a few friends of the poor" appointed a select committee and designated as their agent an Englishman of devout character, Robert M. Hartley, who gave up his business so that he might dedicate himself wholly in his new task to "such labors as the Gospel enjoined and my own convictions required for both the temporal and spiritual advantage of my fellow creatures." Thus began in New York the Association for Improving the Condition of the Poor. This was a citizens' movement. In those early days its leaders and workers came largely from Protestant ranks, but their ministrations were directed toward all human beings in need, of all faiths and nationalities, not merely to their own kind. And so a strong and fine beginning was made for what has continued as non-sectarian family social work in this city.

As the volunteer "friendly visitors" of the A.I.C.P. went down into the Lower East Side, through filthy streets and alleyways, they found families crowded together in dark, stinking tenements, without light, ventilation, or heat, and without the chance for privacy and decency. There was no provision for sewage disposal. Cattle stabled in the city, their horns and tails often actually rotted by disease, afforded the meat supply, and the contaminated milk was watered and doctored with chalk and plaster of Paris. Great epidemics took a high toll. The infant death rate was 275 per 1,000, ten times as high as it is today. Ten per cent of the city's children were roaming the streets in vagabond bands, homeless and schoolless.

Having personally encountered these evils, the leaders of this citizens' movement were not content to stop with individual help and alleviation. They saw the need to eradicate the source of much of this distress. And so, to give a very partial listing, their efforts resulted in the establishment of the first public baths, the organization of dispensaries, the erection of the first model tenement, the enactment of pure-milk legislation, the correction of unsanitary conditions in the city's markets, and the development of a modern city health department and program.

Some decades later another great movement began. It took its inspiration from the original Charity Organization Society founded in London in 1868, which Sir Charles Stewart Loch later headed for thirty-nine years. In the '70s and '80s societies similar to that in London sprang up in several of the larger cities of this country. In New York a group of citizens was again very much concerned about the philanthropic chaos in the city. One of the leaders in the group was Josephine Shaw Lowell, who was a member of the State Board of Charities. She presented the facts to the Board and secured their approval and support for the three New York City members to establish an agency to promote cooperation and improve methods of relief giving. Thus the Charity Organization Society of New York came into being in 1882.

As pertinent to our subject today, it is significant that this new Society explicitly and emphatically declared its freedom from identification with any specific sectarian, political, or national grouping. Its constitution stated (Article II, Section 1):

This Society shall be conducted upon the following fundamental principles: (1) every department of its work shall be completely severed from all questions of religious belief, politics, and nationality; (2) no person representing the Society in any capacity whatsoever shall use his or her position for the purposes of proselytism.

I think it can be stated honestly that through the years these principles have been scrupulously observed by the Society.

At the same time, the constitution stated as the first of six objects of the Society that it should serve as "a center of intercommunication between the various churches and charitable agencies in the city" in order "to foster harmonious cooperation between them."

Mary Richmond, great leader and interpreter of charity organization in this country, who laid foundations for the profession of social casework, quoted approvingly Sir Charles Loch's definition of charity organization as "love working with discernment." [2] And she wrote:

The real home is a sacred thing and should be made visibly a sacred thing to us by all the sacraments of the church. . . . This great work of the church, the heartening of men through education in the life of the spirit, cannot be subordinated to any other function, however humane. . . . Charity is a great spiritual force. . . . We long to make the loving heart of the world a more effectual instrument for the world's redemption. [3]

These views of Miss Richmond we of today would fully endorse. Since 1939 the former Association for Improving the Condition of the Poor and the Charity Organization Society have been merged into one organization, the Community Service Society, which carries on the principles of its predecessors in its interfaith character and broad human base. Indeed, the application of these principles goes beyond the rendering of service to all regardless of race, creed, or color. The governing Board of Trustees includes members of all faiths, as is true also of the 12,000 annual contributors to its support. And the staff, both professional and clerical, is selected according to the sole criteria of competence and character, so that we have working side by side in our many activites Catholics, Jews, and Protestants, Negroes and whites, and persons of Oriental as well as Occidental national origin. And why not? Human need is the lot of us all and we can unite in our common desire to serve mankind wholly on the basis of the individual's ability to do so. From my own personal experience over many years in this setting, I know of

[2] Mary Richmond, *The Long View,* Russell Sage Foundation, New York, 1930, pp. 36, 82.

[3] *Ibid.,* pp. 78, 115.

nothing that can more rapidly and effectively further the American way of democracy, nothing that can better serve the needs of this world, than to bring together in genuine team-work persons of different origins and faiths in the common service of mankind.

Today, as throughout their history, non-sectarian agencies are positive, not negative, in their attitude toward religion and the Church. They uphold and they apply a code of human and social values and of principles for the good life that harmonize with the fundamentals upon which our best religious concepts are founded. There is no basic conflict here and there is no reason for it.

And yet let us face it—with many notable exceptions (especially among the great leaders of our faiths) there is a serious lack of understanding between the clergy and the churches, on the one hand, and our professional social workers and agencies, on the other hand. There is no one simple answer that can explain or describe this situation. Many divergent views and attitudes exist among the churches and churchmen.

At one extreme, there may be a projection of the old conflict between science and religion. Many churchmen view the modern professionally trained social worker in a secular agency as a devotee of everything that today's psychological and social sciences have to offer and, contrariwise, indifferent or antagonistic to religious concepts and spiritual forces. At the other extreme, some clergymen are so intent upon incorporating all the latest psychological knowledge into pastoral counseling that they feel quite capable of doing the whole job and see no need to call upon the social agency.

Even clergymen who are not in this last group may feel that the growing emphasis in social work upon skilled counseling of individuals and families with problems other than economic, involving marital and parent-child relationships and other personal and social relations, is invading their time-honored province of family counselor. In a still more down to earth aspect, the clergyman may feel—and I fear with justice many times—that when members of his flock come under the ministrations of a social agency, he and the church and the role they may well play in the whole process are overlooked or ignored.

The lack of understanding works both ways. The social worker on his side may well feel that altogether too many of the clergy fail to reach out and learn about what social agencies in their modern role really have to offer. It is true that such lack of information is all too general—and this is a challenge to social work and its interpretation. Nevertheless the clergyman is not just any person. He stands in a special advisory role to his people, particularly in time of trouble, and he owes it to them to know community agencies and the service they can render. Too often there is unwarranted skepticism about social agencies on the part of the clergy because they do not know them.

In facing these difficulties, I should like to say first, after more than thirty years in social work with a wide acquaintance among social workers, that social workers are certainly not irreligious, godless souls without a sense of spiritual values. For the most part, as I have known them, social workers have active church connections. As to those who make no explicit religious profession, I have known them as being quite generally highly dedicated people, believing in and practicing ideals in harmony with those of organized religion. Need I say, for the social workers in the agencies best known to me, that professionally speaking they are practitioners not of religion but of social work because it is in the latter field that they have been trained, much as the clergyman is prepared for practise in his field!

The problem, then, is largely a practical one. Like medicine, social work and the ministry are both "helping" professions. Without question social workers should bring the clergy more often into genuine partnership in the helping process. And similarly, the clergy should more often call upon the special skills of social workers to serve their people. As with any misunderstanding, the root is in ignorance, each of the other. Many social workers are not concretely enough aware of the extent to which today's clergyman, in his training in the modern seminary and through his reading, is intelligently informed about and concerned with psychological and social aspects of human need. On the other side, a certain booklet by a leading clergyman on pastoral counseling may be all too typical of an erroneous view which still prevails. This booklet, while assuming that counseling on some of the most involved forms of personal and family problems will naturally be undertaken by the minister, states that it is the cases with an economic angle which normally belong to the social agencies.

I can see social workers bristling over that! For many decades—and most markedly since the past depression and the great growth of public welfare and social security—the private social agencies have more and more directed their skills to the prevention and treatment of many kinds of personal and family problems for people of any economic group, with fees paid by those able to pay. It is in this strengthening of the individual's inner resources, as well as those of his environment, to enable him to meet the demands and opportunities of living, and in the strengthening of the best values in family relationships, that the professionally trained social worker feels he can make his most constructive contribution.

There are two concepts that I think can best guide both the church and social work in relations one with the other. The first is cooperation based on division of labor. Each one of us, I suppose, would like to be so skillful as to be able to minister to all of the needs of the human being. But so vast is today's knowledge, so highly developed are today's skills, that such an aspiration is beyond the limitations of the normal individual. So it is of necessity an age of specialization.

This goes for both the clergyman and the social worker. Let us start from the premise that there is far from enough skilled counseling to meet the need for such service among individuals and families. Thus there is ample room and scope for all good counseling and no one profession can claim a monopoly of it. But let us remember that there is counseling and counseling. There are, for example, legal counsel, psychiatric counsel, social-work counsel, spiritual counsel. And each of these in its own way is a delicate operation, calling for its own professional skills which the layman, even though he may be a professional in another area, had best not tinker with. The counseling for which social case-workers are equipped is a skill in itself. One is prepared for it by two years of graduate professional training in a recognized school of social work, plus a number of subsequent years of professional development under skilled supervision on the job. Skilled case-work counseling is not the handing out of advice based on one's intuitions or hunches. It must begin by understanding as far as possible the origins of and reasons for the person's situation in his personality and experiences—a diagnosis. And in the end it seeks to enable the person to decide for himself what is best for him.

Similarly, the clergyman has had his postgraduate training in a seminary and in the school of experience for his specialized duties. He has doubtless had courses in psychology, in sociology, and perhaps some clinical experience, to equip him for what lies within the normal realm of pastoral counseling. It is hardly to be expected, however, that any save the exceptional clergyman will be equipped adequately for some of the more involved tasks in family and personal problems for which the professional social case-worker has been especially trained, while at the same time achieving success in his primary role of serving the spiritual needs of his flock and the community. A highly important consideration here is the social worker's training and experience in evaluating and dealing with the individual's attitudes and emotions not as entities in themselves but in their close relation to the circumstances of the person's family life, housing, health, job, sense of money and use of it, and the like.

The conclusion once again, practically speaking, is that close cooperation based on respect and recognition by each profession of the special knowledge and skills of the other is the relationship between clergy and social workers that will be most productive in the service of human beings. The clergyman in his role as spiritual leader and counselor, as one who stands in a special place of status and influence with his parishioners, has a continuing relationship with the families of his church. His ministrations are with them in good times and bad, in joy and sorrow, and in some of the most sacred moments of family life. The social case-worker stands ready to serve upon call at times of special need or strain or complication. The social worker brings to bear as needed both his own skills and those of others. For he knows—it is his business to know—the many and varied resources for helping that are available anywhere in the community. Believing in cultivating self-reliance, the social worker seeks to step out of the picture as soon as the situation permits.

The second of the two concepts that can best guide both the Church and social work in their mutual relations is that of the rounded personality, the whole man. Our modern problem is to bring our specialties together into a working unity that can best serve the indivisible unity of the human being. Today in the Community Service Society, close team-work among social case-workers, public health nurses, physicians, psychiatrists, home economists, and nutritional and other professional experts is being emphasized in order better to serve the intimately interrelated physical, psychological, and social needs of each individual human being. The more insight we gain about people in working closely with them, the more we become aware that in the last analysis abounding health, genuine happiness, and productive human relations can come only from the inner spirit of a person, his own sense of rightness within himself and with the world.

It is wholly in order, then, from a scientific as well as a religious viewpoint, that in our concern for the well-being of the whole man we who are in social work recognize the importance and the potential of spiritual forces in the human being, and having respect for each person's beliefs, feelings, and desires, encourage him to utilize the resources for spiritual counseling and strengthening that have meaning for him and that are to be found in the clergy of his own faith.

Thus we in the non-sectarian agencies ask the churches to look to us to assist when problems among their parishioners fall within our area of competence, just as we would call upon pastors and churches as resources needed in the very important area of things spiritual.

What I have said bearing upon division of labor and the concept of the whole man as keys to good understanding and working relations between churches and social agencies would, I suppose, apply in large measure as well within the two great religious faiths which have established their own social agencies, as they also have been concerned with the development of professional social work through graduate training.

As regards the field of Protestantism, there is the further question that has been raised from time to time as to whether the Protestants also should develop a full range of social agencies under sectarian auspices. On this point, as a Protestant myself, I can only express the hope that the great forces of this faith will continue to follow their time-honored tradition of strong support of and reliance upon the broadly conceived and broadly serving community agencies of non-sectarian character, which their Protestant forefathers were so largely influential in founding.

On this point I can best cite the editor of this series, who has given such thoughtful and distinguished leadership to the cause of a united and forward looking Protestantism, F. Ernest Johnson. In his book, *The Church and Society,* Mr. Johnson emphasizes the point I have previously made when he writes:

We have here a problem of division of function and of cooperation based upon such division. It is my conviction that the conduct of social services by the church, broadly speaking, is not the normal expression of Christian social motive. As the institution pre-eminently responsible for teaching ideals and attitudes, keeping faith alive and inspiring to high endeavor, the church can function best by impregnating social work and all other community functions with its purposes, its vision, and its courage. . . .[4]

These stirring words recall to me something else that Mary Richmond wrote:

The church furnishes us with the motive for all our work; it heartens us. We are prepared to give method. . . . But method and motive have need of each other. . . . For centuries charity has looked to the church and must continue to look to it as the uncontaminated spring in the hills, the source of its power. The church, on the other hand, will find the charitable agencies . . . a modern convenience, if no more.[5]

I was thinking about these words as I sat in church one Sunday morning, listening to a moving sermon by my own minister, in which he urged Christians not to retire within the contemplative

---

[4] F. Ernest Johnson, *The Church and Society,* Abingdon-Cokesbury Press, New York, 1935, p. 145.

[5] Richmond, *op. cit.*

life, but to take positive action toward overcoming prejudice and in-justice and toward meeting the human needs of the day. In its ability to give the individual a faith with which to face these troubled times and to provide the motive power for a better life and a better social order, the Church stands preeminent. From religion came the primary motivation for the social agencies we have today. From religion, too, have come those great beliefs we hold in common: respect for the dignity and rights of the individual, awareness that man does not live by bread alone, the urge to develop man's inner resources and capacities toward a better and a fuller life. What greater benefit to mankind could the churches render than to fire the spirits of men with a new zeal for good works that would find expression in some-thing going far beyond the all too lukewarm support now given to these services for humanity?

Can we not, do we not—clergy and social workers, churches and social agencies—speak a common tongue as we work toward the goals of the brotherhood of man and the Kingdom of Heaven on this earth? Do we not come wholly together, for example, in our concern for the family as the paramount human grouping in its meaning for and imprint upon the human being? Are we not equally concerned that the home should have in its housing and neighborhood the kind of physical environment in which the best fruits of family living can flourish? Are we not equally concerned that parents should give of their best to their children, not alone in material things but in unselfish love and devotion, in the cultivation of the best principles of social behavior and of the spirit as well as the mind? In short, is it not in methods and skills that we differ rather than in these basic objectives?

Indeed I know of no common ground where churches and social agencies might more rightly come together to make common cause than in the protection and strengthening of family life. It never fails to impress me deeply when the basic truths of life and religion com-ing out of the wisdom of the ages are strongly confirmed by findings of the latest scientific studies. Such is the case in the scientific data which John Bowlby, psychiatrist of the Tavistock Clinic in London, has assembled for the World Health Organization of the United Nations, and published in his book, *Maternal Care and Mental Health.*

We have always believed that the kind of family life or lack of it which the growing child experiences, fundamentally determines how that child will turn out in life. Believing it so completely, we have done all too little about it. Now Bowlby, after assembling and analyzing researches on child development and behavior from many countries of the world, reports conclusive scientific evidence that it is essential for mental health and social competence that the infant and young child should experience a warm, intimate, and continuous relationship with his mother in which both find satisfaction and enjoyment. The more complete deprivation in this respect is in the early years, the more isolated and *a*social the child becomes. Bowlby states:

. . . The origin of adults' being unable to make effective family relationships is not infrequently itself the result of their having been deprived of a normal home life in their own childhood. Thus the investigator is confronted with a self-perpetuating social circle, in which children who are deprived of a normal home life grow up into parents unable to provide a normal home life for their children, thus leading to another generation of adults unable to do the same for theirs.[6]

The proper care of children (he concludes) deprived of a normal home life can now be seen to be not merely an act of common humanity, but to be essential for the mental and social welfare of a community. For, when their care is neglected, as happens in every country of the Western world today, they grow up to reproduce themselves. Deprived children, whether in their own homes or out of them, are a source of social infection as real and serious as are carriers of diphtheria and typhoid. And just as preventive measures have reduced these diseases to negligible proportions, so can determined action greatly reduce the number of deprived children in our midst and the growth of adults liable to produce more of them. Yet, so far, no country has tackled this problem seriously. Even in so-called advanced countries there is a tolerance for

[6] John Bowlby, *Maternal Care and Mental Health,* World Health Organization, Geneva, 1951, pp. 82, 83.

conditions of bad mental hygiene in nurseries, institutions, and hospitals to a degree which, if paralleled in the field of physical hygiene, would long since have led to public outcry. The breakup of families . . . is accepted without demur. The twin problems of neglectful parents and deprived children are viewed fatalistically and left to perpetuate themselves.[7]

Do we need to look further for a common cause, indeed a great crusade, in which both churches and social agencies can carry into human life their deepest convictions? If it is human personality and human relations we seek to improve, then obviously the place to begin is to see that families are held together through good health and good housing, but even more fundamentally by bonds of love and ties of the spirit.

Yet in New York City alone there are over 15,000 children separated from their families, being cared for in foster, boarding, and institutional homes, not to mention the thousands of neglected and delinquent children coming before the courts. Divorce rates are high, separations frequent, domestic discord rife. Too often the home is without the spiritual, religious, social, and affectional roots which give the sustenance that the developing child above all requires.

This is a charge against us and a charge upon us. How many homes would not need to come to the point of break-up if the strengthening and helping forces of the churches and social agencies could be more fully mobilized to prevent it! Likewise how many children of today might be helped to become the good parents of tomorrow rather than neglectful and depriving ones. Someone has called the spiral a circle with ambition. Thus instead of the vicious circle of inadequate parents whose children turn out to be inadequate parents, we may well see an upward moving spiral of good and ever better parents in each generation.

Indeed, salvation depends upon it—upon the sustenance we can give the family and, through the family, the children. Whether we think of religious, social, or world salvation, do they not go back to the individual and does not the individual in the basic molding of his character and personality go back to the family?

[7] *Ibid.*, p. 157.

Yes, we need more power to do these things we know we must do; and for use of that power to create in human beings the will to make this a better world, social work—like education, government, medicine, and other great fields of endeavor—looks above all to the unparalleled force of true religion.

VII

RELIGION AND CHILD CARE

BY

KATHERINE F. LENROOT

*Formerly Chief, Children's Bureau, United States Department
of Labor*

Child welfare, more perhaps than any other branch of modern
social work, is closely related to religion. Whether one considers historical developments, present-day administration, or the basic philosophy underlying social services to children and youth, one is struck
by both the direct and the indirect contribution of religious people
and organized religion to the protection and care of children.

Both Judaism and Christianity derive from their earliest origins
their concern for children. More than any other of the ancient peoples
of the Mediterranean world, the Hebrews were concerned with the
future of the race and the historic mission of generations yet unborn.
God's promise to Abraham, that in his offspring "all the nations of
the earth shall be blessed," [1] Jesus's admonition to His disciples,
"Suffer little children to come unto me, and forbid them not; for of
such is the Kingdom of God," [2] are examples of the values placed on
childhood in these great religions.

Although my subject has been phrased as "religion and child
care," I should like to broaden the meaning of the phrase to include
the concern of religion for the general well-being of children, as
well as for help for those who are especially disadvantaged by reason
of adverse home conditions or their own individual handicaps. Thus

[1] Genesis 18.18.
[2] Luke 18.16.

97

the phrase, in modern terms, includes social services for children in
their own homes; supplementary child-care services, such as day-
care for children whose mothers are employed; full-time foster care
in institutions or family homes; adoption services; services to unmarried mothers and their children; and services to children who are
emotionally disturbed, mentally deficient, or physically handicapped.
Closely related to these programs, which include case-work and often
institutional or foster-family care, are group-work services for children and young people who need special opportunities for fellowship
in play, camping, sports, or hobbies, or in activities for mental and
spiritual development. Community and state-wide planning and coordination of services for children also constitute an important part
of child welfare, in its broader sense.

It is an axiom that in serving a child one must consider all aspects
of his welfare and development. Hence, close relationships must be
developed among social, health, religious, and educational services.
The fact, moreover, that the home and the family have the primary
role in the care and training of the child, means that family welfare
and child welfare work must be interrelated, and that work with
the child must include services directed toward the strengthening and
upbuilding of family life and parent-child relationships.

Motivation and Inspiration for Services to Children

It is essential that religion continue in the future, as in the past, to
give motivation and inspiration for services to children; that it help
to build a strong philosophical and religious foundation for child-
welfare work; that it aid in efforts to recruit and train young people
for this service; that it reach out to groups most in need of and
farthest removed from services usually available in a well-ordered
community; that all child-caring services under sectarian auspices or
with a religious orientation constantly test their programs by the
best we know of the ways in which children develop healthy personalities and the most progressive experience in organizing and
guiding services for children; and that the relationships of such work
to services under public and voluntary non-sectarian agencies be care-

fully formulated, with full regard to the needs of the general community.

The primary function of religion is the development in men and women of the capacity to relate themselves to God and to their fellow men. To love God, to love thy neighbor as thyself, were the two great commandments of Jesus. Jane Addams, writing in 1910 of "Youth and the City Streets," said:

This, of course, has ever been the task of religion, to make the sense of obligation personal, to touch morality with enthusiasm, to bathe the world in affection—and on all sides we are challenging the teachers of religion to perform this task for the youth of the city.[3]

In the early days of the Christian Church, there were no means of providing care for the poor and the sick, the children and the aged, other than through the Church itself. It is reported that in the earliest centuries of the Church, the "Bishop's House" was the refuge of the poor and afflicted.[4] In the United States, the Ursuline Sisters in 1729 provided in New Orleans the first institutional care for destitute children in what later became the territory of the United States. The Bethesda Home for Boys near Savannah, Georgia, was founded in 1740 by a Methodist, George Whitfield, acting on the suggestion of Charles Wesley. A newly ordained Sunday preacher at the almshouse chapel at Blackwell's Island was responsible for the organization of the New York Children's Aid Society in 1853. It is interesting that the first program of the society was "to district the city so that every ward might have an agent who would act as a friend of vagrant children and arrange street and indoor Sunday meetings for boys."

The accounts of early services for destitute and orphan children abound in examples of organizations started under the impetus of the concern of church people—ministers and laymen—for "destitute, vagrant, and exposed children," as they were described by the Boston Children's Aid Society. This agency was organized in 1865 for the

---

[3] Jane Addams, *The Spirit of Youth and the City Streets,* The Macmillan Company, New York, 1910, p. 156.

[4] Marguerite T. Boylan, *Social Welfare in the Catholic Church,* Columbia University Press, New York, 1941, p. xi.

purpose of "providing temporary homes . . . and of providing for [the children] such other or further relief as may be advisable to preserve them from mortal sin." The originator of the important "Children's Home Society" movement in this country was a young minister, Martin Van Buren Arsdale, who said in 1882, "I have found the way I am going to do my work. The Bible tells us God setteth the solitary in families." His child-saving work was begun by lecturing and taking up collections for homeless children. He received under his protection neglected girls who were cared for at first in his own home.[5]

Extensive services for children under Jewish auspices have, likewise, been developed with motivation similar to that responsible for Catholic and Protestant child-care services.[6] It has been stated that of all the peoples of antiquity the Jews alone made the care of dependent children a special duty under forms of law. In the United States both the institutional care of dependent children and child-placing work under Jewish auspices developed early. The Hebrew Benevolent and Orphan Asylums were established in New York in 1832; the New Orleans Jewish Orphans' Home in 1855.[7]

The influence of religion extended far beyond the establishment of child-caring programs under church auspices. Catholic, Protestant, and Jewish leaders were responsible for the calling and findings of the 1909 White House Conference on the Care of Dependent Children. Large numbers of church people urged the establishment of the United States Children's Bureau, which was authorized by Act of Congress in 1912. The 1940 and the 1950 White House Conferences on Children included religion in their deliberations and recommendations. A large number of leaders in Jewish and Christian work for children participated actively in the 1950 Midcentury White House Conference on Children and Youth. In its follow-up program

[5] Emma O. Lundberg, *Unto the Least of These*, D. Appleton-Century Company, Inc., New York and London, 1947, pp. 76–83.

[6] See *History of Child-Saving Work in the United States*, Report of the Committee on the History of Child-Saving Work, Twentieth National Conference of Charities and Corrections, Chicago, June, 1893, p. 161.

[7] W. H. Slingerland, *Child-Placing in Families*, Russell Sage Foundation, New York, 1919, pp. 27, 37.

in the final Fact-Finding Report of the 1950 Conference, we find the following:

Religion, in its finest expression, is not just one among the interests and experiences of life. Rather, it permeates all interests and experiences and determines basic attitudes, relationships, motivations, standards of value, goals, and conduct in all phases of living. The religious individual's faith regarding the nature of God and his response thereto determines in large measure both his view of the meaning of life and his daily purposes and conduct.[8]

Philosophical and Religious Orientation for Child-Welfare Work

The direct and indirect influence of religion on the development of organized services through which society expresses its concern for children, is an outgrowth of philosophical concepts and ethical principles that are essentially religious in their nature. It is an important function of religion to contribute in each generation to the philosophical foundations upon which the superstructure of child-caring work is erected.

Judaism and Christianity alike view man as the child of God—a God Who knows and cares for each one. This being so, all of us have a responsibility, not only for ourselves and our own children, but for others within reach of our compassion. All, like ourselves, owe their existence to a common Father and stand under God's judgment and in need of God's mercy and forgiveness. With the shrinking of distance in the modern world, love of one's neighbor becomes a matter of world-wide as well as parochial concern.

Along with this concept of a common origin and a common allegiance is the concept of the freedom and dignity of the human personality, the result of the endowment of man by God with freedom of the will and of conscience. In striving to protect and care for God's children, we must at all times be guided by the aim of allowing them to develop their own individual capacities and powers,

[8] *Personality in the Making,* The Fact-Finding Report of the Midcentury White House Conference on Children and Youth, edited by Helen Leland Witmer, Ruth Kotinsky, Harper & Brothers, New York, 1952, p. 211.

growing toward full freedom to direct their own lives, and to take responsibility for themselves and for others—responsibility which is the obverse side of the coin of liberty. All that we do, moreover must take into account the importance of maintaining parental responsibility and conserving family ties.

Whether our concepts of social action are worked out within the hierarchical principle of organic unity in carrying out the Church's mission of charity, under the guidance and direction of the Pope, or a governing body, or bishops, or in accord with the congregational principle of the priesthood of all believers and the autonomy of denominations or of local churches, all religions in our country stress the responsibility of the free individual in relation to his God and to his fellow men. Moreover, the fundamental principle of the freedom and worth of the human personality is acknowledged by many whose religious and philosophical ideas are non-theistic, as well as by those who hold to a theistic foundation for faith, thought, and life.

These principles need to be examined and applied, both to the ways in which services for children are planned, organized, and administered, and in relation to the nurture, training, and development of the children to whom they minister.

In advocating basic security and equality of opportunity for children and youth, we have sometimes, perhaps often, overlooked the primary need in child development of fostering the freedom which goes with the fact that each child is a unique personality. Nor have we always stressed the awakening in the young person of a growing sense of responsibility for the conduct of his own life, for the achievement of his own aims, and for the succor and nurture, in time, of that which he has generated.

In setting goals, we have emphasized greatly the physical, mental, and emotional growth of children, but we have often failed by example and in teaching to give them a sense of "at-homeness" in a universe in which God is, or acceptance of a vocation which has value because it is linked with God's purpose. Children who lack the security of the love and care of a good home need the strength that comes from such a faith and the purpose that derives from such a commitment, more than do others who are more fully protected, loved, and cared for.

Recruiting and Training Young People for Work with Children and Youth

The relative scarcity of well-trained social workers is one of the most limiting factors in the expansion of social work under both public and private auspices. The Committee on Social Work in Defense Mobilization, in which representatives of several national agencies participate, has developed excellent material for use in recruiting social workers. Church organizations and church-related agencies can do much to bring to the attention of parents and young people the possibilities and opportunities in this field of human service

Church-related institutions, like other organizations of this kind, are beginning to recognize the need for special training courses and institutes in child development and social service, for cottage parents and other auxiliary personnel. The Methodist Board of Hospitals and Homes, for example, conducts institutes for house mothers. Many workers in church-related institutions and agencies attend institutes provided as part of the program of the regional conferences held each year under the auspices of the Child Welfare League of America, as well as similar programs under other auspices. This is one of the most important ways in which child-caring organizations can help their staffs to improve their services to children.

The expansion of child-welfare services under departments of public welfare, especially in rural areas, has been greatly stimulated by the Federal aid for such services available through the Children's Bureau under Title V of the Social Security Act. Some church-related agencies and institutions provide similar opportunities for young staff members to receive professional training in social work. It would be helpful if further means could be provided to insure a greater supply of professionally trained children's workers.

Services to Children Conducted under Denominational or Church-related Auspices

The origin of much of our modern child-caring work in church or church-related groups and individuals has already been pointed out. A considerable percentage of all children under the care of children's agencies are being served in organizations under sectarian or church-related auspices.[9]

A large percentage of all the children under care of child-caring institutions and agencies in the United States are receiving care under sectarian auspices. An experimental census of dependent children in thirty-one States and the District of Columbia, made as part of the preparation for the 1930 White House Conference on Child Health and Protection, showed 98,355 children reported on July 1, 1930, as under the care of institutions and agencies conducted by sectarian organizations. This number constituted forty-seven per cent of all the children under such care in the area reporting. Fifty per cent of the institutions and twenty-three per cent of the child-placing agencies in the area were under sectarian auspices.[10]

The 1948 roster of Catholic children's institutions in the United States comprised 288 children's institutions, seventy-two maternity hospitals and infant homes, eighty-nine protective agencies, and thirty-five institutions for various types of specialized care of handicapped children. Major emphasis in Catholic social work appears to continue to be focused on child care. There has been a shift from congregate to cottage type institutions, and from institutional to foster-family care. By the end of 1948, 218 Catholic day-care centers were reported to be in operation.[11]

[9] The term "church-related" is in need of definition. The Department of Social Welfare of the National Council of Churches of Christ in the United States of America is studying this and other matters in connection with a study of services for children, families, the aged, etc.

[10] Emma O. Lundberg, *Child Dependency in the United States,* Child Welfare League of America, Inc., New York, 1933, pp. 55, 60, 82.

[11] Thomas Gill, "Catholic Social Work," *Social Work Year Book,* American Association of Social Workers, New York, 1951, pp. 81–83.

The Council of Jewish Federations and Welfare Funds reported in 1953 over seventy child-care agencies under Jewish auspices, many of them representing mergers of family and child-care services, or family agencies which have taken on child-care functions. With the development of public services, emphasis on preventive services, and improved economic conditions, there has been a downward trend in the number of children cared for by Jewish agencies. Increasing emphasis is reported on treatment for maladjusted children, bringing counseling and adjustment services to wider groups, and development of more intensive case-work treatment supplemented by psychiatric care. Use of large congregate institutions has decreased, with an increase in the use of small, highly individualized institutions to supplement foster-home facilities.[12]

It is difficult to ascertain the extent of child-caring work under Protestant or church-related Protestant auspices. This information will doubtless be furnished in the comprehensive study of all Protestant social work being made under the auspices of the Department of Social Welfare, National Council of Churches. Only a few illustrations can be given here. Figures for day nurseries are not included.

The Methodist Board of Hospitals and Homes reported in 1954 fifty-seven homes for children and eight homes for youth and deaconesses.[13] In the previous year the National Lutheran Council, Division of Welfare, reported over ninety child-care and child-placing agencies, institutions, and temporary shelter or receiving homes under Lutheran auspices.[14] The Protestant Episcopal Church reported in 1955 some sixty-seven institutions and agencies for child care, and a number of youth-serving, counseling, and referral agencies.[15] The

---

[12] Martin M. Cohn, "Jewish Social Work," *Social Work Year Book,* 1951, p. 260; Directory of Jewish Health and Welfare Agencies, Council of Jewish Federations and Welfare Funds, New York, June 16, 1953. See also *Social Work Year Book,* 1954, pp. 287–288.

[13] *Institutions Affiliated with the Board of Hospitals and Homes of the Methodist Church,* Chicago, 1954.

[14] Correspondence with Ann Zophs, Administrative Secretary, Division of Welfare, National Lutheran Council, March, 1956.

[15] List furnished by Department of Christian Social Relations, Protestant Episcopal Church, 281 Fourth Avenue, New York 10, N.Y.

Presbyterians reported thirty-five children's homes, thirty-three child-placement agencies, and two child-referral agencies.[16]

Beverley M. Boyd, formerly the executive director of the Department of Social Welfare, National Council of Churches, wrote as follows in 1951:

Today many of these institutions have added casework service to their programs. The trend for many is to become study homes, with casework placement of children in foster homes. A few are engaged only in case-work; others are day nurseries, nursery schools, or secondary schools for underprivileged children, making use of casework to assist in adjustment of the child and his family. Some agencies and schools provide the service chiefly for children of their own denominations or for those whose families are willing to have them become members. Others determine their intake policy on the basis of need alone.[17]

In a report of the Division of Welfare Agencies of the Presbyterian Church in the United States of America (1950), it was stated that Presbyterians have been leaders in creating and supporting non-denominational or interdenominational agencies. Unmet needs that should challenge the attention of church people were listed as counseling services, institutional care for problem children, services for physically and mentally handicapped children, service for children of minority groups; facilities and staff in rural areas; enough trained social workers. Recommendations for every Presbyterian institution caring for children included, among others, compliance with State regulations; membership in local health or welfare councils; careful consideration of present services and whether there are additional needs in the community which the institution is equipped to meet; consideration of employment of trained case-workers. Pending clarification of child-welfare needs, it was urged that funds should not be used to establish new institutions in communities not

---

[16] *Directory of Welfare Agencies Related to Presbyterian Churches in the Continental United States,* 1953, prepared by the Division of Welfare, Board of Pensions, Presbyterian Church in the United States of America.

[17] Beverley M. Boyd, "Protestant Social Work," *Social Work Year Book, op. cit.,* 1951, p. 352.

now so served, but that such funds as may be available should be used for the support of children in foster homes, temporary placement in institutions, or counseling services. If a new institution was needed, Presbyterians were urged to join with other churches and agencies in developing a community institution rather than a Presbyterian home.[18]

The need for providing national means for exchange of experience among church-related institutions and agencies, and for bringing the work of these agencies in contact with other efforts to serve children and promote their well-being, has led to the establishment of welfare divisions or services in the national headquarters of a number of Protestant denominations, and to the establishment of the Department of Social Welfare of the National Council of Churches. The objectives of one of the denominational divisions represent fairly well, it would seem, the objectives of all. They are:

To mobilize Lutheran health and welfare resources; to strengthen and coordinate the services of Lutheran interbody agencies, relating their program to the total health and welfare programs of the local community, state, and nation; and to represent Lutheran welfare work before coordinating and integrating national voluntary and governmental agencies.[19]

Relating Sectarian Services to Community Needs; Maintaining and Advancing Standards of Care

Several basic questions must be asked and answered from time to time if children's services under church-related auspices are to be of the greatest value. Among these are the following:

1. What are the greatest needs of children in this community? To what extent are they being met? Are the programs of children's agencies and

[18] John Park Lee, Director, Division of Welfare Agencies, Board of Pensions, Presbyterian Church in the United States of America, Witherspoon Building, Philadelphia 7, Pa.

[19] Division of Welfare, National Lutheran Council, *Christian Social Welfare,* October, 1953.

institutions geared to change their focus and emphasis with changing needs? Under their existing programs and objectives, are they now serving a valid purpose? How can their resources and personnel be used so as to contribute the utmost possible to the development of the children in their care?

2. Are children's agencies and institutions related closely enough to family welfare and mental health services, so that children are removed from their own homes only when it is impossible to help them in their relationships to their own families to such a degree that they can remain at home?

3. If child and family services are combined in a single agency, is there sufficient specialization to safeguard the child who is facing the most difficult problems of removal from home and placement in a foster home or institution, or who for other reasons needs the special help of a worker with extensive experience in understanding and dealing with children?

4. How can the work of superintendent, case-workers, and other staff of an institution for children be so integrated as to permeate the whole institution with understanding of each child in his family and institutional relationships?

5. How can the program of the institution or agency maintain standards found by experience to be essential to effective work?

6. What is the responsibility of the children's institution or agency in regard to State licensing requirements or regulations?

7. What financial arrangements should be made for children who are public charges?

8. To what aspects of child development can a church-related institution or agency give especially effective service, as compared with agencies under other auspices? How fully is it meeting its opportunities and obligations with regard to the religious life and development of the children under its charge?

9. How can the experience of church-related institutions or agencies contribute to programs of religious education and religious development of children under other forms of care?

A children's institution or agency desiring answers to some of these questions can find help from the planning and coordinating work of the local council of social agencies; community surveys made from time to time; child-welfare divisions of State departments of public welfare; the United States Children's Bureau; the Child

Welfare League of America; and the national offices of denominations and federations.[20]

The Department of Social Welfare of the National Council of Churches has issued a *Statement on Standards and Licensing of Church-Related Institutions for Sheltered Care*. In this statement, the licensing of voluntary institutions by State governments is generally approved, provided that the freedom of the churches and other private groups and agencies to enter into these fields of service is protected. Standards are recognized as valuable instruments to improve current practise.

A number of church-related institutions and agencies for children are members of the Child Welfare League of America. This is a federation of 270 agencies and institutions which serve children and whose work conforms to standards and requirements for admission to membership recognized by the League. Consultation and advisory service, publications, surveys, and regional conferences are included in the League's program. A study of the program and functions of the League and its relation to other national non-governmental agencies, including national denominational agencies, is now being made. Ways by which the League and agencies under religious auspices can work even more closely together for the attainment of common objectives—always an important feature of the League's program—are being explored.

Church-related agencies frequently receive children on commitment from courts or placement by welfare departments, under arrangements by which public funds pay part or all of the cost of care. Most people believe that such reimbursement should be on a *per capita, per diem* basis. Relationships between public and private agencies in the care of children have been the subject of a consider-

---

[20] A note on the localization of church-related social work seems relevant here (Ed.).

The corporate policies and activities of national denominations regarding social work, to quote Dr. Roswell P. Barnes (*The Activating Concern*, National Council of Churches, New York, 1955):

may or may not be discernibly reflected in the work of the local organizations of the respective denominations. The major portion of the service of the local church is to its own constituents and its own community. The sum total of the social welfare work of all the local churches is vastly more significant in terms of the bulk of service rendered and the impact upon society than the work of the national organizations of those churches.

able amount of discussion, sometimes marked by great difference of opinion. It is important that these relationships be based on concern for the special needs of each individual child, and on maintenance of the integrity of both public and private agencies, with encouragement of cooperative relationships between them.

Special studies need to be made of the ways in which institutions and child-placing agencies provide for the religious nurture and development of the children under their charge. This becomes especially important when problems of children with serious emotional disturbances must be dealt with. It is usually thought desirable to relate the children to the churches of the community. Under such a plan, it becomes very important that the pastor and church school or young people's staff of the local church be given special help in understanding and meeting the special needs of the children, and have an opportunity to influence, in turn, the whole program of care. The need for a religious worker to be recognized as participating with staff representing other professional backgrounds in counseling with and planning for children, including decisions as to the placement of the child in a foster home, would seem to be very great.

The Out-reach of the Church to Children Most in Need of Service

There are many children in our country who are not within reach of the care or protection that they urgently need. In some instances an extension of church-sponsored programs is indicated. Frequently the help of church people in establishing services under non-sectarian voluntary or public auspices is needed.

One of the best examples of the out-reach of the Church is found in work among the children and young people of migratory agricultural workers, carried on through the Division of Home Missions of the National Council of Churches. These programs include Sunday schools and religious services, day nurseries for children whose mothers work all day in the fields and until late in the evening, and recreational activities.

There are many aspects of child welfare that have not been

touched upon in this paper. Juvenile delinquency, for example, is mounting. Its causes are multiple and complex. An attack upon it must be geared both to the individual and the family, and to community agencies and community conditions. Consideration of the delinquent child leads back to the neglected and emotionally disturbed child, and forward to the whole subject of crime. Here the Church's influence is greatly needed. It must operate chiefly through the participation of church people in general community and civic affairs.

Parents of physically handicapped children, parents of retarded and mentally deficient children, need special help and consideration.

The increasing emphasis on pastoral counseling and on family-centered programs of religious education should be especially helpful in these as well as in other aspects of child welfare.

Beyond all special child-care programs, the times call for renewed emphasis on the religious mission of the Church and the personal responsibility of church people. The issues of our era center upon the nature of man and his relation to God. Only as our children are prepared, by love, example, guidance, and instruction, leading to deepening of religious insight and release of spiritual power, can the responsibility of religion for the oncoming generation be met.

VIII

RELIGION AND THE AGED

CATHERINE LEE WAHLSTROM

Formerly Associate Executive Director, Department of Social Welfare, The National Council of Churches of Christ in the United States of America

Religion, through Hebrew and Christian writings from the earliest times, has stressed the importance of the care and protection of older people.

The literature of Judaism as contained in the books of the Old Testament and in the Talmud stresses respect for age and the responsibility of all to care for the older person. "Honor thy father and mother," from Old Testament times to the present, has been closely observed by Jews.

Christianity, with its roots in Judaism, has also emphasized responsibility for care of the aged. In both, the motivation is basically religious; *i.e.,* a belief that man is a creation of God and that man's destiny is divinely ordained.

The Roman Catholic Church presents two examples of organized work in the care of the aged that originated a long while ago and are still operating effectively today. These two religious orders, among many whose self-sacrificing love bears witness to their concern for the aged, are the orders of St. Vincent de Paul and the Little Sisters of the Poor.

St. Vincent de Paul founded in Paris about 1650 an almshouse with accommodation for forty old men and women. One historian says that this institution "pointed the way to what was required and had . . . a human warmth and a supernatural charity very far removed from the cold-blooded official (and officious) aid which the poor so very *rightly* loathe." [1] This same characterization marks the work of the Society today in its institutions for the aged.

The Little Sisters of the Poor, started by Jeanne Jugan of France, has grown until it operates approximately fifty Homes for the Aged in this country alone. The Order was brought here in 1868, when it opened its first Home in Brooklyn, New York. Other Roman Catholic groups caring for the aged are Sisters of Charity, Mercy, St. Joseph, and Divine Providence, and the Felicians, Carmelites, Dominicans, and Franciscans.

Protestants early started institutions for the aged in Germany, in Scandinavian countries, and in England. A deep religious motivation has inspired Protestant churches to establish homes for the custodial care of the aged. As a result, today there are approximately 375 to 400 Protestant homes for older people in this country.

A number of conferences on the aging have been held under Protestant auspices. The first National Conference on Protestant Homes for the Aged was held in 1948 and a similar one in 1950. In 1953 an International Conference on the Churches and Older People was held in Wisconsin, publishing *The Fulfillment Years* as its report. The National Conference on the Churches and Social Welfare (Cleveland, 1955) included this field of social services in its program.

The Department of Social Welfare of the National Council of the Churches of Christ in the United States of America publishes material in the field of the aging, such as *The Congregation Serves Older People, Add Life to Their Years,* and the statement on *Standards and Licensing of Church-Related Institutions for Sheltered Care.*

A two-year study of the Church's ministry to older people resulted in the book *Older People and the Church* by Paul B. Maves and J. Lennart Cedarleaf.[2]

[1] Theodore Maynard, *Apostle of Charity, the Life of St. Vincent de Paul,* The Dial Press, New York, 1939.

[2] Paul B. Maves and J. Lennart Cedarleaf, *Older People and the Church,* Abingdon-Cokesbury Press, New York, 1949.

National Conference on the Aging

The historic interest of the American churches and synagogues in the care of the aged is summed up in this statement from the 1950 National Conference on the Aging sponsored by the Federal Security Agency:

In the first half of the 19th century, both Christianity and Judaism began in this country the establishment of institutions for the care of the aged in the United States. This type of service has developed in both church and synagogue until today there are approximately 800 to 900 institutions under religious auspices. They have a population at present numbering approximately 60,000, with a staff personnel of about 7,000. Demonstrably, then, the churches and synagogues have been working in this field and are making a valuable contribution.

The Religious Section of the Conference adopted this concluding statement:

Religion tells us that our own life is never completely our own but is a stewardship from God. Consequently we honor that life as something extremely precious. It is lived out in the limitations of time and space, but its implications are timeless and universal.

We respect the life which is in our keeping in all its stages from infancy to old age. We respect the life of other people.

In our responsibility to God there is also a responsibility for and toward our fellow man. We are our brothers' keepers.

So we have a respect for the older years of a person's life. For in each person, no matter his chronological age, we see our common heritage, the image of God.[3]

Statistics on the Aged

The aging have, for the first time in history, become a numerically significant group in our total population. More than three-quarters of a million persons are over eighty-five years of age. People are living longer than ever before, because of great medical advances. It has

[3] *Man and His Years,* Health Publications Institute, Inc., Raleigh, N.C., 1951.

been said that we are living in the "golden age of medicine." With the development of the antibiotics many diseases are now either cured or controlled. About one-eighth of our population have celebrated sixtieth birthdays. In 1900, there were a little over 3,000,000 persons in the United States aged sixty-five and over, while in July, 1955, there were 13,700,000 persons who had passed their sixty-fifth birthdays.

This large group of mature persons in our population today constitutes a challenge to the Church. Older people with all kinds of problems need special services. There are the shut-in, the isolated, the handicapped, who need friendly visiting services. The person who is fearful of the future wants spiritual counseling to help develop a faith that sustains. The lonely person who wants affection needs companionship and new friends. The recently retired person asks help in planning an enriching retirement. The older person who wants to do something worth-while can find satisfaction in church service projects. The person with a small pension needs budgetary assistance, inexpensive recreation, and an opportunity to earn a little. To the one who has held responsible positions, the Church should offer substitute satisfaction. The aging person who suffers from personal maladjustments needs counseling and case-work services. The older adults who want to be active and to "belong" can find satisfactions through church group activities, hobbies, and service projects. And to all older persons who find life empty and yet have a "spiritual hunger" the Church offers a special religious ministry.

So, in many churches and synagogues are to be found many types of older persons, from the ones serving as revered teachers of religion or active leaders in many phases of church life, to older adults who feel useless and "not needed." In between these two extremes are the aging persons who face many losses: loss of family, work, status, health, or income.

Does the Church recognize these needs and is it doing something about them? Unfortunately, the answer is often negative for many churches. Too many are only "youth-centered" and either indifferent to or ignorant of the interests and problems of their older members

John Park Lee, Director of the Division of Welfare Agencies of the Presbyterian Church, sounds a warning note here:

Old age does have its problems but it is not in itself a problem any more than is infancy, adolescence, early maturity, and middle age. There is danger, real danger, that we become so obsessed with the difficulties that we forget the great contributions older people can make and are making to our common welfare. We can avoid this danger if we never forget that older persons are not problems, but people.[4]

Trends and Developments

What are some of the new developments in services to the aging in which the institutions of religion are active? These trends fall under four major categories: 1. Homes for the Aged; 2. group programs; 3. services to individuals; 4. community plans.

Homes for the Aged

In the Homes for the Aged tremendous changes are taking place. Among these are better, more attractive, homelike surroundings; single rooms replacing dormitories; change from separation of the sexes to living arrangements for couples; transition from large, institution-type buildings to bungalows, apartments, separate living quarters with community lounge and dining facilities. The change in usage from "inmate of the institution" to "resident" or "guest of the Home" implies recognition of each person as a human being entitled to privacy and loving, intelligent, individualized care.

Religion makes an important contribution to Homes for the Aged through the chaplains. They do more than conduct a ministry of worship; they offer a vital ministry of individual counseling and spiritual guidance. To quote from *Add Life to Their Years:*

Homes, as far as possible, should secure chaplains who have had clinical training so they can serve the deep needs of older people. Anxiety, loneliness, guilt, and fear are at the base of much illness and maladjust-

[4] John Park Lee, "Not Problems but People," *"Social Progress,"* March, 1951, pp. 6–9.

ment. Trained chaplains through skillful pastoral counseling have aided greatly in the therapeutic and rehabilitative development of many aging persons in Homes and Hospitals. Qualified chaplains are trained to work as a team with caseworkers, physicians, group workers, and other staff members concerned with the person's individual needs.[5]

Unfortunately only a few Homes in the country are able to find chaplains with this specialized clinical training; but more courses are being given today in seminaries, to help future ministers and chaplains understand the needs and problems of older people. There is a great need for further development here.

Jewish agencies have led the way in adding case-workers to their staffs in Homes for the Aged. They interview applicants, counsel older persons before and after entering the Home, and assist them in adjusting to their new living conditions. Unfortunately the majority of church Homes do not feel that they can afford case-workers. The Federation of Protestant Agencies in New York has helped many of its affiliated Homes for the Aged to meet this financial problem by pooling their resources and having several Homes share a case-worker among them. This plan has proved most satisfactory. It is as important for Homes for the Aged to employ trained caseworkers who can help older people with their social and emotional problems as it is to employ doctors and nurses for their physical ills.

One new development that is really pioneering is the psychiatric program developed by Dr. Frederic D. Zeman at the Home for Aged and Infirm Hebrews in New York City. His staff—a psychiatric social worker and three psychiatrists on part time—is making an invaluable contribution to our understanding of the aging.

Only recently have recreation and creative activities been considered important in the life of the aging person. It was not until the late 1930s that the care of the aged moved away from the traditional Western concept that to be aged meant to be old and exhausted. Today, there is growth toward a more dynamic concept of aged persons, that they should spend their time in happy, useful, effective activities.

Today in our better church Homes we find an enriched activity

[5] Department of Social Welfare, National Council of Churches, *op. cit.*

program, including craft classes, discussion groups, social activities, physical therapy, attractive lounge and recreation rooms, beauty and barber shops, occupational therapy, residents' planning councils, creative hobbies, infirmary programs, important service projects, and rehabilitation services. Where there is no employed staff to develop an activity program (and there are even fewer Homes employing group-workers than are using case-workers) various plans are used, with Board and volunteer leadership, utilizing skills and talents of the residents themselves. Sometimes several Homes cooperatively employ an occupational therapist or recreation leader.

Homes for the Aged are changing rapidly also in the matter of payment by the residents. Until recently—and it is still the case in many Homes—men and women were required upon entrance to give to the Home their entire savings. For this lump sum they were promised care in the Home for the rest of their lives. Loss of independence and insecurity resulted for the residents; many did not even have spending money, except as the Home would dole out small amounts to them. From the standpoint of the Home also, life-care payment has not been satisfactory. As one superintendent said, "Mrs. W. has been in our Home for twenty-seven years. When she came she gave $600 which was supposed to pay for her room and board, health care, clothing, etc., for the rest of her life." That story can be multiplied thousands of times all over the country in our church Homes where the initial life-care payment was used up many years ago.

Today the trend is toward a monthly payment plan based on contributions from the resident's Social Security or Old Age Assistance grants. In this time of transition, however, many older persons do not have Social Security and many are too reluctant to ask for public assistance; so the Homes struggle to care for their residents with inadequate budgets and dwindling resources from investments and contributions.

Some of the church Homes for the Aged are opening their facilities to older people living in the community. Those persons can take part in social, vocational, and recreational programs in the institution and enjoy its facilities, such as the library, lounge, and craft shop. The Lutherans are suggesting that older people from the neighborhood might come to the Home for personal consultation and even for a hot midday meal. For too long there has been a cleavage between community church and Home. With doors opening, better services can be provided both ways: to the aging within and those outside the institutions.

In recent years there has been a growing awareness of the need for increased infirmary services in Homes for the Aged. Since residents enter at an advanced age, there is need for more facilities for the sick and chronically ill. In the past and at present, by and large, the conventional Home for the Aged has limited itself to accepting only the so-called "well" person. If Homes for the Aged are to continue to meet the changing needs they must have a more liberal policy of admitting the physically infirm and a more nearly adequate program for their care.

There has been a trend toward keeping people *out* of Homes as long as possible so that the Home can be reserved for those who require congregate care because of emotional or physical needs. One of the most widely known services is that of the Non-resident Aid Program, initiated in 1945 and developed by Mrs. Ruth Laverty at the Peabody Home in New York City. As the pressure for admission by an increasing number of applicants became more urgent, the Home sought ways and means to care for more elderly women than the maximum capacity of the Home would permit, without spending huge amounts of money for additional buildings, equipment, and maintenance staff. In addition to already long waiting lists, they found that many women were applying and being received in the Home long before they needed or really wanted to enter, because they were afraid that there would be no place for them later.

The Home for Aged and Infirm Hebrews in New York and the Brooklyn Hebrew Home and Hospital also offer a non-resident program. Patterned somewhat after the home-care program of hospitals, they offer case-work regularly and on call. The worker counsels with the older person in his home, helping to solve personal problems, finding part-time work and more suitable housing, and arranging for medical examinations or assistance in obtaining old-age benefits. If there is need, visiting nurse service and a visiting housekeeper are provided. Recreational and social programs are included. With these specialized services the individual needs are taken care of, thus enabling the older persons to remain independent much longer.

2. Group Programs

In the second area, churches and synagogues are achieving significant developments in group activities. Older people are being served through various forms of recreation and informal education. Development is quite spotty; in some parts of the country a great deal is being done, while in other sections the Church has not awakened to its possibilities. For example, in New York City there are sixty-two non-profit clubs and centers, with a membership of 9,265 older people, according to a directory published by the Welfare and Health Council of New York City.[6] But of these sixty-two clubs only a handful are located in churches or are sponsored by religious groups. Many churches are still so completely "youth-centered" that they neglect their older members.

Raymond M. Hilliard, former director of the New York City Welfare Council, urged churches to establish centers for the aged. He said: "In view of the rising age level of the population, the great demand for such centers cannot be met by the city and social agencies alone."[7]

Many churches have facilities that are idle most of the time. Even busy churches have rooms that are free in the mornings and early afternoons while children and young adults are in school or at work but retired people are free to come. Also, churches have volunteers and latent leadership that can be called upon for work with older people. It takes less staff time than group activity with young people, since the past experiences and abilities of the aging themselves can and should be utilized.

Probably the most common group activity for older people in the church is the weekly adult Bible class, with its occasional party or social programs. Many churches are now feeling that this is not suffi-

[6] *Directory of Recreational Facilities for Older People in New York City,* Welfare and Health Council of New York City, New York, May, 1953.

[7] *"New York Times,"* March 21, 1953.

cient to meet the needs of aging persons who find that time hangs heavy on their hands and are often lonely and bored. To serve not only the growing number of older people in the congregation, but also those in the community, many churches are starting clubs, hobby groups, day centers, and informal education classes.

One church in Ohio reported that its most recent development has been the establishment of a Day Center with facilities for older persons as a home away from home. A large house, empty for years, was leased, and a complete refurnishing job was undertaken. Volunteers from the congregation contributed the labor, and furnishings were supplied by the local Lutheran Women's League and by many individuals. It is announced that a full-time worker will soon supervise the regular use of the Day Center as well as the decentralized program.

While in most cases it is wise to have separate groups for older people, every effort should be made to integrate them into the total program of the church. Older people need association with others having the same interests and problems, but they should never be made to feel that they are an isolated group or that their days of usefulness have ended.

Group activities including both men and women have proved most successful. Some clubs, because of their programs and interests, however, have limited their membership to either men or women alone.

The setting of a minimum age has proved a stumbling block in some places and has limited the participation, since many men as well as women are sensitive about their ages. For this reason there is a trend toward choosing names that do not designate age alone, although such names are still popular, for example, Golden Age Club, Senior Citizens' Group, Three Score Club, and the like.

One lady said, after a joyous church recreation program: "If I had known what fun it is to be old, I'd have wanted to be old sooner!" A church leader writes: "One might ask, 'Who are the aged?' 'Not I,' states emphatically the spry old lady of ninety-two who hasn't missed a church party. 'Nor I,' declares the white-haired woman of seventy who was not a guest but a hostess at the last church picnic."

Those church groups that tend to stress church or service projects, such as religious programs, missionary sewing, home visitation, etc., usually are limited to older persons from the church membership. Today, as indicated above, there is a growing trend toward opening the doors to all aging persons in the community. Some of these community clubs or centers are started and sponsored by the church for everyone, while other organizations use church facilities but are led and promoted by civic groups. There is increasing awareness that the church has an obligation to serve the aged through its facilities, leadership, and program.

A workshop on Group Activities for Older Adults, led by the writer at the International Conference on the Church and Older Persons in Wisconsin, July, 1953, listed the various types of activities in a well-balanced program. These would include: 1. religious and inspirational features, such as worship services, choirs, etc.; 2. informal educational and cultural programs such as book reviews, travelogues, group discussions, film forums; 3. service activities through the church or some community agency; 4. social, recreational programs such as parties, picnics, trips, games, sports; 5. the arts—music, crafts, dramatics, hobbies.

The workshop also agreed that good group-work principles should be used with older people as with younger. Some of these principles are: know the members of the group, their interests, hobbies, backgrounds; allow the group to organize itself and to plan its own program; keep the program flexible and change as interests change; use community resources; center the program around persons, not activities; do not be over-protective of older adults in program activities; spread responsibility widely in the group; be democratic, patient—do not try to move too fast with older people.[8]

Educational activities in various forms have been sponsored by churches and synagogues. One popular lecture series was on "Preparation for Retirement and Later Maturity." The topics have included such practical ones as budgeting, nutrition and health, hobbies, religion, pensions, Social Security, etc. The Federation of Protestant

[8] *The Fulfillment Years in Christian Education,* National Council of the Churches of Christ in the United States of America, New York, 1953, p. 29.

Welfare Agencies in New York has developed Program Ideas Exchanges, Training Courses for Older Leaders, Come See Tours, etc., for older people in the area.

Camping, one of the new recreational services for older persons, has been developed extensively under Jewish auspices. Also, for a number of years the Methodist Church has sponsored summer camps, conferences, and regional meetings for older people. Their large attendance testifies to the need they are meeting. The importance of an older adult committee for every local church has been stressed.

3. Services to Individuals

The third area in which the Church is active is in individualized services for older people. Foremost in this field, the Church offers a religious ministry and pastoral counseling. Worship services, observance of religious holidays, daily devotions, singing of familiar hymns, Holy Communion, and other religious observances mean a great deal to older people who have had a religious background. Apparently those who have had deep religious experiences earlier seek the comfort and inspiration of the Church even more as they grow older.

The religious counselor plays a significant role in meeting the emotional needs of the older person. The late Reverend Paul L. Tilden, Associate Director of the National Council of Churches' Department of Pastoral Services, said:

Many older people are alone in the world and suffer greatly because they feel "nobody cares" what becomes of them. Often such people are the victims of anxiety—a continuous state of fear which in time inflicts disastrous effects upon the personality, as well as upon mental and physical well-being. In older people, these fears generally center around feelings of unbearable loneliness, uselessness, and financial uncertainty. A positive approach on the part of the spiritual counselor can impart a sense of security to persons such as these.

Unfortunately, some pastors cannot help older people because they have not the patience to listen to their problems, or because they fear or resent old age themselves and have not worked out a satisfactory religious philosophy for their own later years. One of the greatest needs today in the field of the aging is the formulation of a positive religious program. All programs should be deeply rooted in a spiritual philosophy. With the great increase in gerontological literature dealing with health, housing, employment, recreation, etc., there is a great dearth of adequate material on religion and the aging process. Seward Hiltner, Paul B. Maves, and others have written significantly on the subject, but there needs to be more literature giving a sound religious orientation and base for this important topic, meeting the need for greater recognition of the development of the spiritual life in older people.

One group of individuals that needs special services from the Church is the sick and chronically ill. Those who are in bed or at least house-bound need much help which the Church can supply. In order to meet these needs, Friendly Visiting Service has been organized in many churches—calling on the sick, writing letters for them, securing new glasses, shopping and doing other errands, giving home-maker service, relieving their "adult-sitters" so that they, too, can have recreation and relaxation. In Chicago and other cities churches are recruiting volunteers, and Family Service Agencies are training and supervising them for specialized work with the aged infirm. This is a service that has great promise for the future, especially when churches and social agencies work together.

Housing is an area of special need for many older persons. The Foster Home Program is designed for elderly people who prefer to live with families. The task is to find desirable boarding homes which afford family life. Social workers know the difficulty of getting adequate foster homes for children and it is proving even more difficult to find homes for the aging. However, with more public education and an awakened interest in older people, church families are being persuaded to open their homes. The Jewish Community Service of Nassau-Queens in New York has pioneered in the Foster Home Program. One local Council of Churches is planning to produce a film which will encourage church members to take in older people to live with them.[9]

---

[9] Without any "program," this was once a rather common practise; it may still persist in communities where "baby-sitting" has not become general.

The Immanuel Congregational Church of Hartford, Connecticut, has tried to help in the matter of housing by donating two apartment buildings. These were given to the church many years ago, in trust for the use of widows, by some friends who specified that the rentals be kept very low. Other churches are struggling with the problem of providing houses where men and women may have private rooms but may eat together. A small but helpful service by some churches is a registry of available rooms for rent.

Anyone who has tried to find appropriate quarters for an elderly person on a small retirement income and in questionable health knows the vast need for nursing homes and similar institutions whose fees are not exorbitant. A few churches are now operating nursing and convalescent homes to help serve the growing number of chronically ill.

As a pastor is often called on to give counseling in fields of health, part-time employment, financial matters, emotional problems, housing, etc., it is important for him to know when to refer the person to specialized social agencies. Some of these problems are deep-seated and need long time case-work services. Some churches and denominations have set up their own case-work agencies, such as the Episcopal Service for the Aging, in New York.

4. Community Planning

Very little will be said here about this area of service for older adults, except to emphasize the importance of cooperation by church and synagogue with community agencies in social-welfare planning for the aged. Some cities have made community surveys and written recommendations, and are developing long-term projects for older adults. Churches should always be included in such community planning, and the clergy should work with physicians, civic leaders, social workers, psychiatrists, economists, and others, forming a team in planning for the aged. The Community Chests and Councils report that 166 cities now have planning groups for older people on a community-wide basis. Most of them have religious leaders serving on the councils. This is wise, for ministers have much to give as well as to gain from cooperative planning. In Cleveland, a city-wide committee plans a weekly, interdenominational Sunday afternoon vesper service for older persons. The committee also helps to arrange transportation for those who need it.

On the national level religious leaders are cooperating with others through such coordinating groups as the National Committee on Aging of the National Social Welfare Assembly. Pastor Francis A. Shearer of the United Lutheran Church served as chairman of a committee comprising many religious leaders of the three major Western faiths which produced two outstanding volumes on the aging, *Standards of Care for Older People in Institutions.* Pastor Shearer is also chairman of the Committee of the Aging of the National Council of Churches' Department of Social Welfare.

Some of the national church groups specially concerned with the problems of the aging are the Council of Jewish Federations and Welfare Funds, the National Jewish Welfare Board, and the National Conference of Catholic Charities. A number of the Protestant denominations have active programs on services to the aging; notably, the Methodist Board of Homes and Hospitals, the Department of Christian Social Relations of the Protestant Episcopal Church, the National Lutheran Council through its Division of Welfare, and the Division of Welfare Activities of the Presbyterian Church.

Religion has made and is making a significant contribution to older people. However, there are many churches that are unaware of or indifferent to the programs that are being developed for the aging. Much remains to be done. In this era of social awareness, churches have a unique role to play in meeting the challenge, responsibilities, and opportunities of serving older people.

IX

SOCIAL WORK IN A CITY PARISH

BY

ROBERT W. SPIKE

Pastor, Judson Memorial Church

Seventy years ago the minister of a comfortable East Orange, New Jersey, church wandered through the streets of the Greenwich Village section of old New York. He was there because the papers were filled with accounts of the vast waves of Italian immigrants that had rolled in upon the city and were settling in that area.

He was greatly moved by the poverty and the tragedy that faced these new Americans. His name was Edward Judson, and he was the son of Adoniram Judson, who may be called the founder of the Protestant foreign mission movement in this country.

Edward Judson had been born in Burma, but had been raised and educated in Hamilton, New York. He already had a secure reputation as a learned man and a preacher of distinction, but this visit to the Village changed the course of his life. He was a Baptist; so he looked around for a Baptist Church in the neighborhood and found the Berean Baptist Church at the corner of Bedford and Downing Streets which was a small middle-class church, whose families were already beginning to move away because of the settling of the new immigrants.

As soon as the church was without a pastor, and that happened before long, Judson made known his availability and was immediately called to its leadership. The church gave every evidence of being doomed. Hence the missionary concern that had captured Judson's father and many members of his family before him found a new focus in this home mission field. Moveover, his concern was not limited to a narrow evangelistic effort, but embraced the whole social situation in which the immigrants were caught.

He immediately started a program of visitation which resulted in his involvement in a complex of problems. A program of services centered in the church was the response to these problems. For example, a cooperative woodpile was started, because the flats were heated by wood and the people had difficulty getting it; an employment bureau was set up. For a period this church and the political clubs were the only agencies interested in the welfare of the new immigrants in the area.

In 1892, Judson's leadership had so proved itself that he was able to get financial support to erect a new building on Washington Square, and the name of the church was changed to the Judson Memorial Church, in honor of his father. The new building was an imposing structure designed by Stanford White, with John LaFarge and Augustus St. Gaudens contributing to the interior decoration of the sanctuary. The new plant expanded the opportunities for social service: sewing schools, gymnasium, kindergarten, medical services.

At the same time, the traditional program of the Protestant Church was being carried on, although during Judson's lifetime little aggressive evangelistic work was expected among the Italians, who were nearly all Catholic. So this program differed greatly from the pattern of much of the other Protestant work carried on at the time. Many families did join the church, but this was almost completely on their own initiative. Many more were involved in all the various phases of the program. How much the motivation for the extensive social-welfare program of this church lay in the hope of making Protestant converts is difficult to assess. Certainly the fact that many converts were not made disappointed many of Judson's early supporters. He died in 1914 under the great pressure of trying to finance an enterprise that was too large for its constituency.

I have given some history of the early years of Judson to illustrate rather graphically the most general attitude among American Protestants toward urban social work; that is, that the crowded inner city is a mission area which necessitates social work, and it is closely bound up with the winning of converts. This was particularly the case in the early part of the century, but in nearly every city which is just beginning to discover its inner-city problem this is still a typical Protestant response.

In the case of Judson in its early days, the services were highly paternalistic and benevolent. There were great human needs growing out of poverty, disease, language barriers, crowding, unemployment; and the church gave to meet these needs generously and sought to enlist the gifts of others. Symbolic of the whole spirit of the Judson Church in those early days were the three outdoor ice-water fountains at the corners of the property; they provided a neighborhood that was without refrigeration some relief in the hot summer months. The traditional program of the church was intermingled with the social services.

The second phase of Protestant urban work was marked by a trend toward a greater division between the religious life of the church and the social services it rendered its community. That is, it became more truly an institutional church. In the case of Judson, the medical service separated itself and became a completely independent agency. The recreational activities were less tied to the on-going organizations of the church. An Italian and an English congregation went their separate ways. A large part of the social group-work program was separated from the church and moved into a neighborhood house closer to the center of the Italian population.

Other social agencies had developed in the community and were doing a far more comprehensive job of working with all age levels and providing solutions to a great range of problems.

It was in this era that the profession of social work generally began to develop its standards and to open up the vast reaches of case-work, group-work, and counseling on a concentrated basis. The institutional churches and church-run neighborhood houses either suffered by comparison because their workers did not have professional training and their facilities were inadequate, or they developed into non-sectarian social-work agencies. Judson's program went partly one way and partly the other. Some projects did separate, as in the case of the medical services, and others limped along, tied to the church.

This is the kind of situation that led many Protestant leaders to take the position that the church had little business doing social work *per se*. It seemed that the churches ought to be devoted to the full-time proclaiming of their religious message and to dealing with people on the deeper levels of their spiritual needs. For the past two decades, some Protestant leaders have been saying that churches should support and encourage community-wide social agencies. They should send their laity into secular agencies and insist that they get the best possible training.

There have been good reasons for this. Social work that is just a cover-up for proselytizing does little good for any religious cause, and it must be understood that in the case I am discussing the newer residents were not Protestant. Moreover, social-work programs that were not evangelistically aggressive still retained the disadvantages of under-paid staff and lack of training in social work generally.

And so the great vision of Edward Judson came finally to this point: a dwindling recreational and social program that worked with a constantly decreasing group. The Neighborhood House was closed; many of the Italian families moved to the suburbs, and the recreational work was carried on by outside groups using the facilities of the church.

It was to this situation that the New York Baptist City Society, which was the parent body of this church, addressed itself shortly after the Second World War. The Greenwich Village community had grown to be well established and extremely self-reliant in three generations. The Bohemian quality of the Village, which had been typical of it in the 1920s had become altered by the more anonymous way of life of the midcentury creative intellectual, but there was still a large local population of young professional people. New York University had grown into the largest university in this country and completely surrounded the church. Several neighborhood houses and churches were located in the community, and through the years the church had lost touch with its neighborhood.

Under new leadership, a small corps of people set to work to discover a relevant ministry for the Judson Church in Greenwich Village. They began with a strong theological base, with a conviction that classical Reformation Protestantism had an authentic word to speak and to contribute to this cosmopolitan microcosm which is the Village. This was a word of the integrity of the divine judgment upon all the myriad ways of our living. The ministers and the new group of people who were attracted to this experiment saw that the usual kind of preaching and traditional church program could never accomplish this end. The whole attention of the church in the past five years has been directed toward throwing its resources into solving the knottiest problems facing the community. A full-time student program centering in a cooperative house was the first expression of this intention. The ministers and church members immersed themselves in the political and civic affairs of the Village. The life of the church itself was stripped to the real essentials of worship and serious study. The participation of church people in community affairs was conceived as an act of churchmanship.

The development of all these areas, just referred to briefly, is a subject in itself. However, the social-work program of the church, which is the particular concern of this paper, was looked upon in exactly the same way as the other ministries: the one addressed to students; the one designed for the community as a whole; and the one that we call somewhat facetiously our "mission to displaced intellectuals."

Direct social work was another channel into the life of the community. Protestant churches in cities rarely realize how isolated they are from the really vital concerns of the great bulk of the population. Recreational resources open to the public are one way of pushing aside that barrier. However, simple provision of such resources as the gymnasium, arts and crafts, and dancing instruction, had neither a positive nor a negative meaning for either the church or the impact of the church on the community.

In 1949, the church's community center was being operated by outside social-work groups with no over-all coordination, no purpose, and little plan. The program was largely centered in work with children and young teenagers. Our first two years were spent in the process of observing the needs of the community, getting to know personally all the young people in the center, and in prodding the cooperating agencies into looking more deeply into what they were trying to accomplish. Our program was identical in orientation with those of the other settlement houses in the community, but it had inferior equipment and facilities. We were actually in competition for constituents. In fact, a common remark when we later put our program on a different basis was the taunt, "If you don't do thus and so, we'll go to Sullivan House," or "We'll go to the Bedford Settlement."

We found our special mission almost by accident. A gang of boys had begun their own small reign of terror in our community three years before. In addition to purse snatching, car stealing, drunk-rolling, and robbing dry-cleaning establishments, they caravaned from settlement house to settlement house wreaking havoc. They did not want to become permanently attached to any group, and they could turn any well-organized club into an uproar in no time at all.

They started to annoy the Judson Church Center in precisely this way. Some of the staff reacted with fear and called the police. Some of the ministry of the church saw a peculiar vocation for us with this group of boys. They were convinced that the strict and unyielding use of authority would certainly be ineffective with them.

Eventually a break came with the outside social agency that was cooperating in our program on the very underlying principles of the program. The church decided to go ahead with a limited budget and a strong determination to put into practice an open program based on acceptance and trust.

It was not easy at first. A non-punitive program, when you are dealing with boys who have much experience with courts and police, is always interpreted as weakness. We became the butt of many destructive acts directed against property and some of the personnel. We were fortunate in having staff members who were able to understand the roots of this aggression, to work patiently with each boy, and to remain confident about the rightness of the program in the face of immediate evidence to the contrary.

The real break came for us, in this turmoil, when a group of these boys and their girl friends were apprehended by the police on the roof of a nearby building and accused of a number of robberies. I went to the police station, having been called by the parents of one of the boys, to try to deal with the situation. We happened to know that in this particular case these boys were not guilty of the crime, although they were completely capable of it. However, through much negotiation with the police, after rescuing the leader of the gang from a second beating at the hands of the police in the back room of the station house, we had a group of them released in our custody. This single incident broke the ice with this group of anti-social kids that we were particularly interested in working with, and since that time [1951] the focus and center of our work on weekday evenings has been boys who have police records, or who are too turbulent to fit into the on-going work of a settlement house.

The kind of trust that we were able to evidence in this incident and many succeeding ones, with the members of the staff participating, brought boys from all over the Lower East Side and the Lower West Side to our program. In fact, a policeman said to us a year after we started, as he came in and looked over our group, "Why, you have the rejects from every social agency in Lower Manhattan." We thought it was a compliment rather than an insult.

We began to develop, by trial and error, methods for the kind of program that is essential in working with basically very disturbed boys. Our focus is on the ages between fourteen and eighteen. We learned that you cannot expect to form immediately neatly structured little clubs or interest groups, and that you have to think constantly of short-term interest projects, gradually adding resources to the situation.

The real heart of our work is in establishing satisfactory relationships between a boy and some adult. One of the reasons, we feel, why the boys are anti-social, why they are in trouble with the police, why they are unhappy, is that they have had unsatisfactory relationships with adults. And so our staff concentrates, within the framework of what looks like a fairly typical social agency program, on this kind of direct personal friendship.

We have been in the midst of all kinds of gang fights and riots. I have stood in the middle of our gym and watched fifty boys whom

I had never seen before engage fifty of our own boys in pitched battle with knives and clubs. I had the really rewarding experience of having some of our boys, who had originally been most antisocial, step in beside the staff members and create order out of that situation, withdrawing completely from the battle in which they had started to participate. And in the three years that we have carried on our program, the delinquency rate in the precinct has dropped enormously. There was a time when it was not really safe for a woman carrying a purse to walk in Washington Square Park after dark. We have very little of that kind of trouble now.

Of course, this has led us away beyond the limits of the building into all kinds of referral work and to work in the courts, and into every institution where our boys have spent some time. We have become very closely related to Youth House, which is the detention home for boys in this city. I act as Protestant chaplain there, and the staff of our center cooperates with the staff of the House.

Our work has taken us beyond the young people themselves into their homes. We have begun to try to lift some of the burdens of the adults in the homes out of which these children come.

In our efforts to get support for our program—because it had to be financed with help from the community as well as from the church itself—we have gone into all aspects of social-work financing. The social-work part of the church program has been drawn close to the church itself. We do not think that the present orientation of the program will be permanent, since we hope that this particular situation will be ameliorated in our neighborhood.

We had in 1954 a registration of about 150 boys, and we are in close touch at all times with about forty boys. By "close touch" I mean that we are working on a case in the court, or in relation to an institution, or in the boy's home.

It may be somewhat presumptuous to make generalizations about the nature of social work in urban churches, based on our limited experience. Nevertheless, some very strong impressions have emerged from our experience, and they are offered here for the purpose of exploring the field further and for discussion.

I have mentioned that there are generally two patterns that

Protestant social work has fallen into: one, of the social work carried on within the on-going program of the church, and the other characterized by a sharp divorce between the life of the church and the social-work adjunct.

We have tried to work out a new relationship. The pattern is as yet nameless. This is what seems to underlie it: first, a direct social-work program should be carried on by a church in a theological context. This does not mean that religious content is automatically a part of the program. That depends entirely upon the constituency. In the case of our teenage rehabilitation program, formal religious education would have been divisive, and beyond that, in the early stages, it would have been irrelevant. What this formula does mean is that the program should be understood by the church to be an integral part of its life, one of the ways by which the church lives out the love of God in the community. It should be, as far as possible, removed from the usual connotations we give to the word "charity." The social-work program must not be an adjunct of the typical and "real" work of the church, but in continuous discourse, so to speak, with the other parts of the life of the church. This should result in as much participation as possible on the part of the church members in planning and carrying out the project.[1]

Ideally, trained personnel carrying on the program should have adequate theological and social-work training. More important, however, than degrees from a theological seminary or an accredited school of social work as qualifications for the job, is evidence of a functional and working theology that has insight into and under-standing of the nature of man. That means, in psychological lan-guage, a warm and accepting spirit about all kinds of behavior; and in theological language, an understanding of the sinfulness of all creatures to whom the love of God comes equally and without reservation. These two things must be fused in personality and experience.

A second observation is that a church should carry on direct social work only if this is going to meet urgent, otherwise unmet human

[1] See Horace R. Cayton and Setsuko M. Nishi, *The Changing Scene: Current Trends and Issues,* National Council of Churches, New York, 1955, pp. 137–143.

needs. Duplication of services and competition of effort in this area is shameful. The church has to be acutely sensitive to a sociological perspective on the community—and not just in terms of surveys which reveal trends of population and the percentage of Protestants in it.

Again, the church must be participating in the feelings and anguish of the troubled sections of its community. It is then prepared to work at several levels. One of these levels is that of policy in relation to political and civic groups, aimed at alleviating the causes of social distress. For example, our program of teenage rehabilitation may be made unnecessary some day because of the kind of housing we are trying to get for the community.

Another level is that of social policy in relation to secular social agencies, which aims to undergird and strengthen them and to work cooperatively with them wherever possible. The whole community should work at these trouble spots, for they are the concern of the whole community.

Still another level is that of direct social welfare programming *if no one else is doing it,* to the limit of the resources of the church. The church, if endowed, ought to be more mobile than those institutions that have been set up specifically for social betterment, since the church's vested endowment interests are not confined to one field.

The church ought to be the first to act in the crises of human need, and should then seek to establish on-going means of meeting the need. I have said that we do not conceive of our present teenage program as being forever established. We have thought of it on a five-year basis. The church has to have a parish concern and this parish concern is not limited to the membership or the constituency, but extends to the whole community.

Our third general observation is that the church has a responsibility to secular social agencies. This responsibility is, first, one of support. Contemporary urban society would be a jungle without the department of welfare, hospitals, clinics of all kinds, private and public settlements. I believe that fat, red volume, *Social and Health Agencies of New York City,* deserves a place beside the Bible on my desk, and I do not feel it is a confession of dereliction in my spiritual duties to say that it is used almost as much.

But the church has another responsibility to social agencies, and that is to act as a friendly critic. The professionalization of social work is something for which to be thankful, but it has brought many problems, too. There is a tendency among trained social workers to think that no one has an understanding of the human situation save one of their own group. The church ought to be sympathetic, and to be a sympathetic critic in this area, because the church of all institutions has had the most experience in choking to death on its own private vocabulary!

I had the experience not long ago of being interviewed by a representative of a large social-work federation to which I was looking for aid for our project. In trying to describe to her some of the underlying assumptions of the program, I rather automatically fell into the language that is used in social-work circles. She said to me, "By the way, are you a trained social worker? You speak the language so well."

We ought to be able to help break down professionalism when it gets in the way of human understanding. We ought to be able, too, to help personalize those vast social-work institutions, and to try to interpret what they really are doing to those who are using them. There is nothing more frightening than to sit in a clinic hour after hour beside someone who is trembling with fear, wondering what is going on behind those closed impersonal doors. And we ought also to be able to interpret to social workers the effects of encrusted institutionalization on people.

What I really am trying to say is that the church has to be in the stream of living humanity that flows through our streets and the only way for the church to do this is for churchmen, laity and ministers, to go where the tough problems are, openly and without fear. The demurrer may be, yes, but if you do this the more truly religious functions will have to suffer. This I deny, for these functions, whatever they may be, are meaningless if they are not done in a living relationship to the people among whom one is set. More than that, the religious message has meaning only when the historic faith comes to grips with the roots, and not the symptoms, of the contemporary crisis.

Social work in an urban church must inform, and be informed by, that confrontation—otherwise, it has no reason for being.

X

COOPERATION BETWEEN MINISTERS AND SOCIAL WORKERS

BY

THOMAS JAMES BIGHAM, M.S., S.T.M.

Instructor in Christian Ethics,
The General Theological Seminary

Cooperation between ministers and social workers is so eminently desirable, so very reasonable, and not impracticable, that it might seem almost unnecessary for us to do more than note the fact. After all, everywhere men of goodwill believe in cooperation in this world of competition and conflict. The clergy are outstanding proponents of unity, peace, and concord; and the constant concern of social workers is to enlist all members of the community to work together in helping those in need.

It seems then that ministers and social case-workers would form a natural partnership in helping with personal problems, for both intend to help individuals and families achieve the inner strength which makes them at once individually self-reliant persons and socially responsible members of the community. While their methods of working toward this goal are in many ways diverse, it is common to both that they must in their own persons be fitted to help, for personal relationship in its symbolic depths is of the essence of pastoral work and of social case-work. Moreover, social work has a religious background in our culture. The concern for social welfare expressed in the great ancient terms, *zedekah, agape, caritas,* is a continuing force of living religion today. And, not least, on the clearly practical level, dependency, delinquency, and disease raise many problems for the solution of which the minister and the social worker each needs to call on the special skills and resources of the other in the interwoven problem of the spiritual and moral and of the psychological and social. F. Ernest Johnson tells us, for example, that when Mary Richmond published her book *What Is Social Case Work*,[1] a clergyman suggested to her that she call it *First Aid to the Pastor* and sell it in religious bookstores. Cooperation between ministers and social workers seems both necessary and important.

The sad fact of the matter, however, is that this cooperation at the present time leaves much to be desired. The cooperation which seems at first glance and on the whole to be so reasonable presents us, on only slightly closer examination, with fundamental and far-reaching philosophical questions. We must decide on the nature of science and the more debated problem of the nature of the social sciences; and then also on the supposed conflicts of science and religion. We must have some contemporary understanding of the function and nature of a profession in comparison with, and in contrast to, the religious understanding of vocation and calling. We must ask what is the essential meaning of religion in contrast to the character of irreligious secularism. And, not least, there is the question what it means to help someone find fulfilment in life— not least, for this is the question of the meaning and purpose of life itself.

In this paper the task, then, is first to state some observations and conclusions that lead one to think that these problems need not be insurmountable obstacles to cooperation; then, secondly, to go on to speak of two levels of cooperation in the work of helping persons in need. I confine myself to speaking of social case-work (not of social group-work, nor of social action), partly because here the problems are most urgent and partly because this is what I know most about. And we can consider here the minister only in his function as pastor, for the work of priests, ministers, and rabbis in administration or board membership, in policy-making or fund-raising, or in social research, does not raise questions peculiar to the ministry. It is

[1] Mary Richmond, *What Is Social Case Work*, Russell Sage Foundation, New York, 1922.

pastoral work that is the unique responsibility and privilege of the ministry.

I

The troublesome fact about interrelating the work of the pastor and that of the case-worker is that every reason for cooperation cited above raises problems of how two can walk together except they be agreed. Occasions for cooperation present obstacles to it. On the practical level there is ignorance in each profession about how the other goes about its work, and why this is so. One or the other may wonder why it is that intake may be closed, or a pastor may not call on someone in another parish; why privately arranged adoptions are without benefit of investigation, or why a Baptist baby may not be baptized. These are some instances where misunderstanding is easier than understanding.

Such misunderstanding leads to suspicion of foolish professionalism or of unrealistic dogmatism; or it may confirm one's opinion that the other profession intends to be meddlesome, mothering, dictating, forcing an opinion which can always find illustrations enough in fiction and in fact to give it the air of realism, and the pretense that it is not a prejudice. Or the prejudice may attach itself to the fact that different types of personal fitness in the helper are required of the pastor and the case-worker. What Karl Mannheim has called the special quality of case-workers, "the impersonal personal relationship" they establish with the client, gives no clear basis for understanding the pastoral relationship with its theistic overtones of suprapersonal judgment and love. Nor does it work the other way around, that the pastor understands the case-worker.

Again, the very similarity of stated goals may be occasion for doubt. It is hard, of course, to see how anyone can disagree with the proposition that "the well-being of the individual and the betterment of society" are desirable, when it is thus stated in general terms. But many disagreements obviously would appear were these goals given particular expression in such problems as these: whether a separation or perhaps a divorce is advisable; whether an Old World wife ought to keep her earnings; or, that perennial question in the work-a-day world, whether a person should play who cannot pay—that is, ought someone on relief to go to the movies? On these points cultural differences and cultural changes, and also the religious sanctions of both, need rethinking.

Basically, all these obstacles seem to arise from the failure of the one profession to give the other professional recognition, to see the other's work in its own terms and to allow it its rightful autonomy. There could be, for instance, a covert note of superiority in the suggestion that case-work is "first aid to the pastor," as though case-workers were trained technical assistants engaged in carrying out a limited part of the pastoral function—as I once heard a cleric describe them. Perhaps this view is to be expected of an old profession looking with kindly misunderstanding at one that began within living memory; but it nevertheless merits the compliment that is returned—the younger profession regards the older as out of date, out of touch, and untrained.

The problem then seems to be twofold: 1. looked at as a matter of the interrelations of two social groups, the fact is that there is not enough meeting between the clergy and social workers to allow for genuine acquaintance and appreciation; 2. looked at in terms of the relationship of their respective bodies of professional knowledge, there is much to be done before case-work thought and theological thought can be related.

While much is still to be done, at present one may at least have a perspective on the problem. The useful perspective is an over-all philosophy that takes account of both modes of thought. It seems to be one such as can be sketched here. On the one hand, there is social case-work theory, *i.e.,* the relatively unbounded and undefined body of scientific knowledge from medicine and medical psychology and the social sciences which, although undefined, is nevertheless focused and brought together in case-work theory; on the other hand, the field of theology in which there is much definition but of a largely unscientific subject-matter. Not that theology is anti-scientific (at least at its best), but that it is pre-scientific and does not intend, even if it could do so, simply to demythologize itself to meet some perhaps passing philosophy of science. Rather it takes the sciences into its prescientific view.

A basic example of this mode of thought is that religion sees the helper of every sort as a manifestation of the prototypal image of the Shepherd of Israel Who leadeth Joseph like a flock and of the Good Shepherd Who giveth His life for the sheep. To the religious mind every empirical observation, every theoretical advance of scientific knowledge, makes this image the more manifest.

Now this over-all philosophy is very theological, and consequently does not appeal to everyone. Contrariwise, for the mind of the social scientist, the empirical observations and the theoretical inductions may be the whole picture, or all that is worth paying attention to. Along this line it can be said that the essence of case-work is to understand and deal with the factors that cause maladjustment, to appreciate individual differences, to see how the family is important for individual life, and to know the interrelations of case-worker and client and to make them constructive. We note how these last phrases describe the function of the helper. These essentials of case-work were greatly strengthened and established by the contributions of psychoanalytic psychology, its insights into the emotional meaning of behavior, its characterization of individual differences, its findings about the function of the family in the dynamics of individual development and, especially, its descriptions of professional-personal relationships in the terms of the transference and the identification which allow for catharsis, insight, and constructive action.

This description of giving help seems a far cry from the image of the Shepherd, but it is not always so. There are three possibilities. First, the psychological description is not alien to those religious minds which do not limit themselves to thinking only about religion. The prescientific view can take science into itself, as we said above, and find in modern psychological terms the ancient words *zedekah, agape, caritas* expressing themselves on a different level for a different world.

Second, this description need not be strange to the mind of the case-worker when it truly is religiously neutral and when it sees the possibility of case-work being given any of several philosophical interpretations. And, in turn, religion can place this case-worker who is religiously neutral within a religious frame of reference. "They serve Him who do not know His Name"—thus Harry Emerson Fosdick has put the religious understanding of this position.

There is, however, a third position. In it a deep gulf is fixed between the religious mind and the scientific mind when that scientific mind is also secularist. Secularism may be defined, not as a denial of religion, but as the denial of its relevance to the major activities of life, regarding the activities of life as self-explanatory and self-sufficient. The secularist does not always deny God; he simply is not interested. His interests are here. In its extreme form secularism makes a religion of this life, or of knowledge about it, often scientific knowledge. It often centers upon practical moralities in the improvement of society and of individuals. It does not necessarily think the faith of historic religion to be irrational; it simply dismisses it as irrelevant. In the Judeo-Christian view, social work seems unguardedly open to such secularism. As a matter of fact, however, Florence R. Day says, "Faith in the dignity and unique worth of the individual and family has always been the focal point of case-work." [2]

But simply because case-work never inquires into what it means by faith, it is quite liable to settle for a philosophy of its autonomy unrelated to anything deeper than the democratic social process. It then tends to become an anti-religious religion which regards the Judeo-Christian faith as irrelevant both to its outlook and to its practical purposes. We reach an extreme when we try to think how the minister and the case-worker who is secularist can walk together. Here there is little meeting of minds. As indicated above, "Except they be agreed," not much ground can be covered, Amos notes. Of course, another translation has it, can two walk together "except they have made an appointment?", for concordats seem a possibility even here.

What remains difficult in this case for the religious person is his feeling that if the religious roots of social concern are forgotten or

[2] Florence R. Day, in the *Social Work Year Book 1941*, Russell Sage Foundation New York, 1941, p. 517.

relegated to the past, they must have been denied or betrayed. This is sometimes so; but often the secularist suffers inherited invincible ignorance. Moreover, the religious mind knows that at some times even one who claims to be a heathen and is an outlander is called to minister according to the Divine purpose. Isaiah records it of Cyrus of Babylon: "Thus saith the Lord thy Redeemer . . . of Cyrus, He is my shepherd." The possibilities of cooperation are very wide, if both be agreed on some immediate destination or if each finds a positive place for the other's thinking in his own philosophy of life.

In accordance with this line of thought certain lines of action suggest themselves:

1. Clergymen and case-workers can profitably explore in group conference case situations that involve cooperation or common problems.

2. Such group conferences could compare basic concepts and learn data of both fields. For example, ministers could undertake to learn what is meant by psycho-social diagnosis, environmental manipulation, insight therapy, the "non-judgmental." Social workers could learn what is meant by creation, redemption, sins and sin, forgiveness, prayer. This is a matter of words and of ideas but also of attitudes. One sometimes notes that "permissiveness" is as frightening a thought to a minister as is, on the other side, the word "sin," which seems to set off unfortunate chain reactions in the case-worker's mind.

3. Each group might participate to some degree in the training experiences of the other: the one perhaps recording and reporting a purposeful interview, the other engaging in both critical study and devotional use of biblical material.

4. Schools of social work and schools of theology might include more of these matters in their studies. Theological schools have a rather better record in this respect. Need schools of social work fear controversial matters so much as to omit study of works done in faith? Should they neglect study of the faiths in our pluralistic society in which these works are done?

5. Each group might learn that there are a number of professions in this world. To hear the clergy talk of the laity or to hear social workers talk of the community, one would often think all laymen

alike. That puts it extremely, for the minister does know that there are the doctor, the lawyer, the Indian chief; and the social worker does know that there are the psychiatrist and the psychoanalyst—and maybe the cultural anthropologist; but this remains a limited recognition. It seems too obvious to say so, but one thing that any learned profession should learn is what the other professions are. Only the multi-discipline approach can clarify many matters.

To sum up these observations of the current situation: we must note that the desirable cooperation which seems so reasonable at first glance involves in fact far-reaching questions of philosophy. We are forced to note that this task is one for which we all are little prepared because of the considerable ignorance on the part of each profession about the other, about its manner of work and its modes of thought. This ignorance can be and often is overcome, especially where theological students and clergy learn more about pastoral counseling and about the contribution case-work makes to training in skills of interviewing, particularly where social case-workers are in agencies under religious auspices or where a chaplain is part of the therapeutic team. Even there, however, little attempt has been made to relate the respective bodies of professional knowledge: the one, the relatively undefined body of scientific and socio-psychological thought; the other, the highly defined body of pre-scientific theology. The meeting of minds is not impossible, but it seldom happens.

In this situation cooperation is difficult. Yet it can be achieved and it remains desirable. To the serious social worker it is desirable because, after all, the person in need—that person on whose dignity case-work focuses its faith—is at once a social being related to others, and a psychological being with an individual dynamic in his own life, and a religious being who would see life whole; and these three dimensions of his unique existence are deeply interrelated and intertwined. And to the minister, or to the case-worker who stands in the Judeo-Christian tradition, this unity of a person's being and the unity which it is given him to have in community with others, both spring from the Highest of unities: "Hear, O Israel, the Lord thy God is one." Because we are monotheists, we can be content with nothing less than seeing the created world in all its diversities as one, as a universe in which all things return to the One from Whom they took their origin—their Creator and their Redeemer.

II

Where there does exist in some degree a meeting of minds and a joining of purposes, cooperation between a minister and a case-worker appears, and this on one or both of two levels.

The first level of cooperation is a working together in which each work is, as it were, outside the other, side by side and supporting each other, but extrinsically. Either the case-work or the pastoral work may be the center of the scene, the other a valuable factor.

The second and deeper level of cooperation is a working together in which the work of each is internally related to the other's, in which attention to the social and psychological dimension of a life process can be, indeed must be, related to the moral and spiritual dimensions of that same process. Here again either social case-work or pastoral work may be predominant, but the other is at hand, not as a flying buttress to the superstructure, but as a necessary buttress in the structure itself.

Examples of the first kind of cooperation come to mind if we simply list the aspects of the pastor's place in the community as seen by the social worker, and then note the aspects of the case-worker's place as that is seen by the pastor. This may be most conveniently explained by a case illustration:

Miss B., fifty-six years, was hospitalized for carcinoma. She had no immediate family, was disturbed about the seriousness of her illness, concerned about convalescent care and about the use of her savings. In working with her on these problems, the medical social service worker learned that Miss B. had been an active church member. She responded readily to the worker's suggestion that perhaps her minister could arrange for her admission to a convalescent home. The minister responded promptly, discussed the entire situation with the social worker, and visited Miss B. several times while waiting for a vacancy to occur in the convalescent home. Miss B. discussed her financial problems with the minister. The medical social worker arranged for a lawyer to draw a will for Miss B.

As a result of the minister's help, Miss B. developed increasing acceptance of her situation, more peace of mind, and her bitterness toward her distant relatives who did not visit her lessened. The minister arranged for a member of the congregation to drive Miss B. to the convalescent home. Other church members called and the minister visited her as often as he could until her death three months later. The medical social worker also arranged for the chaplain in the convalescent home to visit Miss B.[3]

Here the case-worker finds the pastor's functions to be several. 1. To her the minister is a citizen who is expected by the community to take responsibility for helping people in the community. In this case it is he who arranges for admission to the convalescent home. 2. He is the leader of a special social group, and he can call upon the members of that group for volunteer services. Here it is visiting the sick, but in other situations it might be providing foster homes, giving special gifts of money, providing transportation, or acting as interpreter. 3. He is a person with certain privileges in society. Nothing of this comes to notice in this case but it might, for example, if the situation had required pastoral attention to the patient outside the regular visiting hours. 4. He is an authorized religious teacher who, as in this case, teaches truths from the stores of traditional wisdom about illness, fear of death, and bitterness at estrangement. 5. The pastor is a spiritual guide. In a way not unrelated to his work of teaching, as spiritual guide he helps the person, as in this case, to come to see for herself the meaning of accepting illness and of forgiving those that despitefully used her, and finding as a result more peace of mind and soul. These insights are characteristically gained and these consolations found either by some ministry of the Word of Scripture or by administration of the sacramental rites.

In turn, the pastor finds the case-worker to be the responsible representative of a profession with specific skills and knowledge. 1. She has a special knowledge of social and psychological problems. This includes budgetary problems, so that in this case one can only assume that financial problems discussed with the minister were not

[3] *Cooperation Between Churches and Welfare Agencies: Report of a Demonstration Workshop,* Federation of Protestant Welfare Agencies, New York, 1952, p. 9.

very complicated. At least, social case-work has this as a characteristic area of competence which the ministry does not have. 2. She has an extensive knowledge of community resources, in this case apparently knowing what convalescent homes were available and what they were like. 3. Similarly, the case-worker has certain privileged relationships but different ones from those of the pastor—different calling privileges, use of the social service exchange, and the like. 4. She has certain resources of time and of relief money to help in a variety of situations. 5. She can employ the "impersonal personal relationship" of case-worker and client in a constructive manner. And here we may suppose that she also helped to take the bitterness away from one bereft of friends and relatives by means of this relationship and through standing by without emotional involvement.

In observing the types of work the pastor and the case-worker do in this situation we see what extrinsic cooperation means. The work of each is appropriate to the needs of the person and to the situation, each work complements the other, and they fit together without interference. Yet something is lacking which might be of great importance in some other situation. Even in this case we can see some matters that have a double aspect, one in the case-work field and one in the religious sphere.

There is the social problem of loneliness; this is also the religious problem of being alone before God but yet not alone. There is the social problem of bitterness at being deserted by friends and relatives, but this can at its deepest level be met only by the religious solution of forgiveness. There is the social problem of adjustment to disease; but this is also the religious problem of humbly accepting the limitations of our finitude. And we may note that both the case-worker and the minister seem to give the woman the will to live, perhaps just in standing by, communicating to her, as it were, sub-rationally the will to live, and probably by being helpful, giving her super-rationally the will to live nobly. But, in addition, the minister seems to communicate to her the grace to die well.

These situations point to the further kind of cooperation important in many another case where they are articulated. The following case excerpt is an example:

A seventeen year old girl was referred for case-work by the minister to whose parish she was recently come, because she was always hanging around the church, tagging along after him, needing more time than he could afford. The girl gave to the case-worker a recent history of depression with suicidal tendencies. She was staying out of school because she failed in work. She was messy at home and could not or would not clean up her room. Punishment for these disobediences did no good.

On psychiatric consultation it appeared that this was related to her despair over perfection in herself and the need for constant reassurance of others' affection. The causes of this became clear: an orphan of a father who had deserted before her birth and a mother who had died shortly after her birth, she had unfortunately been in a succession of foster homes. One of these, where she had stayed longest and where she had thought she was the real child of the foster parents, was the home of a woman of pronounced religious opinions who denied the existence of evil and insisted on what she thought a biblical "Be ye perfect," a perfection that was to be shown in perfect manners and high grades at school. Although the girl attended other churches herself, this cut deep. She grew to be a "Model Child" but with rebellion inside at having to mother other younger children in the foster home. The death of the foster mother made another change essential, and this precipitated her depression which kept her from school, made her messy about her things, and fearful of disapproval.

She responded to case-work treatment but had an increasing doubt whether it was morally right for her to turn to human beings for help (as she turned to the case-worker and had turned to the parish minister who by this time had been moved to another city). She asked whether she should not turn only to God for inner help, even as the religion of her foster mother had taught her. At this point the case-worker suggested that she discuss this with a minister related to the agency whom the case-worker would familiarize with the problem.

On seeing the minister, the girl poured out a jumbled account of her life ending by saying that "she was tired of taking the blame, tired of pretending to be very grown up, tired of hiding anger under a quiet surface." In depressed tones she spoke of her fear of not being the best in her class, but she brightened up while saying it and laughed when the minister said that St. Peter was not the only Apostle. Then she asked whether it was all right to get help from a human being. "Why not?" the minister said, and, he reports, he thought of two texts: "Except ye become as little children . . . ," and "If ye love not your brother whom ye have seen, how . . ." She explained that in fact she had got more help from her parish minister and case-worker than she had ever got from God directly, and said that God must be working through them. Her case-work relationship became more relaxed and more productive.

The minister also encouraged the new foster parents to ease off on their regime of punishment.

In conference the minister and the case-worker found in this process three points of great importance, each of which has significance in case-work diagnosis and treatment and in pastoral diagnosis and counseling.

First, the girl is exhausted at playing the role of mother's little helper, but finally comes to see that it is all right to be helped. In case-work terms, she is helped by acceptance to be accessible to case-work therapy; in theological terms she is helped to see that she was not created by the independent Creator to be herself an independent creator but to be one among interdependent creatures, or in the plain language she herself used, "God works through people who help."

Second, the girl is caught between pride at being a model child and humiliation at not being first in school. By the emotional support given her by the case-worker and the minister, she is enabled to begin to learn not to think more highly of herself than she ought to think. This moral and therapeutic advance is made possible because of the attitude both case-worker and minister take toward her, attending to her and not centrally to her punishable actions. The case-work principle here is that the therapeutic attitude is non-judgmental (which, it may be noted, receives its most prominent statement in St. Matthew 7.1). The religious principle of this moral attitude is the doctrine that "while we were yet sinners, Christ died for us."

Third, the problem of personality in this girl can be described as a breakdown of a conformity which had been exterior and not interior, and which indeed had been at the cost of inner arrested development. Or, in theological language, it is a problem of works without faith. And the solution may be put religiously: the beginning of a new life of faith with the works that follow after—justification by faith, the case-worker noted.

Here the pastoral work may of course be seen in one way as an external social and religious sanction for obtaining case-work help—an aid, a resource, a flying buttress. But, we must note, religion is implicit in and intrinsic to the solution of the reconstruction of a life. This is clear in this case because the client herself thinks and speaks in religious terms; but it would be true anyway, for these terms are true to the facts of the situation. Not only can case-work and pastoral work *fit onto* each other in extrinsic cooperation, but, under a common philosophy they can *fit into* each other intrinsically. When case-worker and minister know each other's methods of work and basic concepts of thought, and especially when they both hold a theistic world view in which the empirical results of the social sciences have a place, then cooperation can be complete and rewarding.

The relation of case-work and religion is essentially intrinsic and not by chance or patchwork. Life made by God tends toward Him, whether we know it or not. When we know it, the processes and problems of life are explicitly religious (as they are here for client, case-worker, and minister) but they are always at least implicitly so.

These realities make it possible to discuss the deep problems of life in psycho-social terms or in religious terms or preferably in both, for the processes of life are truly both human and divine, and may be recognized as such by both case-worker and chaplain.

These realities make cooperation possible. Especially may this be so today, for case-work with its new psychological insights, and religion today with its renewed spiritual insights, both see that character is more basic than conduct, and that morals and manners are not best dealt with moralistically but understandingly and spiritually.

The highly desirable cooperation of case-work and religion is reasonable and it is feasible. Amid the humdrum of daily practicalities its full dimensions do not always appear, but at times it is given us to see that all things work together for good to them that love God, or, as the clearer words of another translation put it: "In everything *God works* for good *with* those who love Him."

XI

STATE AID FOR RELIGIOUS SOCIAL WORK
The Record of a Panel Discussion

BY

F. ERNEST JOHNSON, Chairman
EDMOND BORGIA BUTLER
LELAND P. CARY
ROBERT MORRISON

The Chairman:

Today we have a novel set-up and one that I think is very well suited to our purpose. The topic is "State Aid for Religious Social Work," which means, of course, the use of public funds by any branch of government for the aid of social work conducted under religious auspices. It has nothing to do with the nature or the quality of the work itself, which may not differ observably from what is carried on under non-sectarian auspices. For purposes of this discussion religious social work designates only social work carried on under religious auspices. We are to consider whether it is proper that public funds, derived from taxation, be used for the support of such social work and if so under what conditions.

This, of course, we all recognize as a form of the church-state question, which is very much discussed these days and sometimes with a good deal of acrimony. It comes to the fore most frequently in relation to education. The issue over Federal aid for education has been greatly aggravated by disputes over the extent to which it is proper for public funds to be used for services to children who attend religious day schools.

This question often arises in connection with hospitals or other welfare enterprises under religious auspices. We have therefore arranged a panel discussion of this issue in order to address ourselves to specific questions that arise in connection with it. Let me introduce the members of the panel.

Edmond Borgia Butler is president of the Superior Council of the United States Society of St. Vincent de Paul. Mr. Butler is the only member of the group who is a member of the bar.[1] Dr. Leland P. Cary is executive secretary of the New York City Society of the Methodist Church, which conducts many enterprises that have social-work features. Mr. Robert Morrison is a member of the staff of the National Jewish Welfare Board.

I suggest that we start with a question that will elicit some basic facts. In what forms does social work under religious auspices actually receive support from public funds at the present time? I am sure that all the members of our panel will have something to say about that. I will ask Mr. Morrison to speak first.

Mr. Morrison:

I should like to make this preliminary statement. My personal belief is that state assistance for social work under religious auspices has always been directed primarily to particular ends, the major one of which is the foster care of neglected and dependent children. This kind of work receives more public aid than any other.

Even as far back as in the 1870s, Kate E. Huntley points out in her book on the financial history of New York City Social Work, rather considerable sums of public funds were allocated to religious organizations doing work with neglected, dependent children.[2]

The second major area in which substantial public financial aid is available to religious agencies is, of course, that of assistance to the sick poor. Here we find subsidies granted on a *per capita* basis to hospitals maintained under religious auspices.

Third, I believe that as far back as 1756 the St. Andrew's Society, which was an organization for the assistance of Scotch immigrants

---

[1] The Editor records with deep regret the decease of Mr. Butler.

[2] Kate E. Huntley, *Financial Trends in Organized Social Work in New York City,* Columbia University Press, New York, 1935.

in the United States, formed a small clinic which received a modest public subsidy for assistance to Scotch indigent poor, and these, of course, were virtually all of one religious group.

The Chairman: Dr. Cary, let us hear from you on this question.

Dr. Cary:

There are a few church-sponsored neighborhood houses that have carried on their work in under-privileged communities. They have, I think, sought to minister to children especially, without any regard to religious affiliation, and in their work there has been no emphasis upon the church's religious education program. It has been a kind of pioneering. I think it has been primarily a means of educating the church to a keener responsibility for these areas.

In these neighborhood houses there have been nurseries, but as the need increased they were not able to function adequately without assistance from the City. Therefore, we now have been receiving in these day-care centers considerable aid from City welfare departments.

Another area in which we are using some public assistance (in this case from the State) is the maintenance of Homes for the Aged. The financial aid makes it possible to care for many more people. These are the two main areas, I think, in which we receive public aid.

The Chairman: Do you wish to add to those categories, Mr. Butler?

Mr. Butler:

First, I should like to clarify the word "support." The assistance of which Mr. Morrison spoke goes back farther than the date he mentioned. The City of New York, with the authority of the State, encouraged the construction of large congregate homes for dependent and neglected children, and also for some delinquent children. It was done in this fashion: the City gave to each of the new corporations formed for the purpose a lease for one hundred or ninety-nine years (a typical long-term lease) to a piece of property for a dollar a year, on condition that an institution of a particular nature would be erected and maintained.

That has been done with religious organizations of different faiths without any discrimination whatsoever. And, as far as I can see, it was a good investment on the part of the government. There are certain basic facts which should be brought to mind before we begin a discussion of this subject. We all know them, but we sometimes forget them.

In the first place, it costs more money to run a government institution than a private institution—and that is not a criticism of government-run institutions. Where you have to operate under law, your auditing alone is one of the big factors, and each expenditure must be legally authorized. I was the secretary of the Emergency Relief Bureau from the time of its formation in 1934 until it was merged in the Department of Welfare on January 1, 1938, and we spent about $535,000,000 during that period.

We were the successors in interest of private groups that attempted to take care of the needs of people caused by what is called the Great Depression. If we operated as government agencies, we had three governmental partners—the City, the State, and the Federal Government—and no one of them would accept the audits of the others. We actually had to have a large space, for which we paid rent, to house the auditors of the State and Federal Governments. The official, Colonel Wilgus, in charge of our Works Division once said that in order to fill out a requisition for a pencil he had to file sixty-seven pieces of paper. That is an exaggeration, but in government operation at its most logical and efficient level the cost is far greater than the cost of a comparable private enterprise. Therefore, by the yielding of a lease, for a dollar a year, on what was then country land, the community was greatly benefited.

The most recent case that comes to mind is that of a property in New York City that was later sold and is now occupied by a public school. When the lease was granted in 1844 the land was worth practically nothing. Nobody wanted it. The property was given to the Institution of Mercy, which maintained a home for children. That piece of land at Eighty-first Street and Madison Avenue couldn't be given away in those days. Today it is extremely valuable.

By this method such various charitable agencies under religious auspices were brought into a field that they were peculiarly fitted for, and were also given money toward the maintenance of institutions; but they received no money for the construction of buildings. For this they had to use their own resources. Moreover, at no time in the history of the City's relationship with any of those child-caring institutions has it actually paid the full cost of the care of the City's charges.

For instance, Mr. Morrison mentioned hospitals. In some hospitals in New York City, the City pays for patients who are a public charge. It pays twelve dollars a day for ward care. In many hospitals it costs twenty-four dollars a day for the same thing. So, when one speaks of public "support," the term is not accurate. It is not support; it is a payment on account, for services rendered.

Remember also that since the Depression and the assumption by the government of large responsibilities in the welfare field there has been a vast change in our tax structure. That was occasioned by the Depression and then by war. The government is left in a position where it takes so much of the surplus money that the philanthropic dollar is said to be disappearing. Therefore, the government, since it takes away from the wealthy money formerly given to charity, must now subsidize; it must replace the dollar that is no longer there.

If a man made a million dollars in 1900, he could give almost all of it away in charity. But if he makes a million dollars in a given year today, he will probably have only a relatively small part of it to give away. Out of that, he must provide for his charities.

The Chairman: Mr. Butler has launched us already into a discussion of the question I was going to raise next, "Under what circumstances is this kind of assistance justified?"

Mr. Morrison:

One additional point which I have not mentioned, and to which neither Dr. Cary nor Mr. Butler has referred: State and local assistance is also given for special education in social-work agencies under religious auspices—Americanization classes, classes for the blind, and for the hard of hearing. In other words, assistance is given for a definite educational program that would normally have to be carried out in the City schools, but in which pioneer work has been done, with public assistance, by many of our social-work agencies under religious auspices.

Mr. Butler:

Might I add to that? The new ventures of the private agencies here in New York City, Protestant, Jewish, and Catholic, for emotionally disturbed children—Children's Day and Night Shelter, Ittleson Home, Astor Home, and one (presently without a name) projected by the Protestant Council—represent an altogether new function. The City government is not able at the present time to put up the money for these buildings and their various facilities, but the private agencies have stepped in and said: "We will furnish the plants and facilities if the City will make us a payment"—in this instance about eleven dollars a day per client in contrast to the three dollars and a half a day normally paid.

The Chairman:

If I get the drift of this discussion you are saying that the justification of public contributions—let us accept Mr. Butler's amendment here as to "support"—toward the cost of maintaining these services is that such services have to be rendered by the community in one form or another, and if they can be appropriately and less expensively provided by this or that group, then it is quite proper for the public treasury to make some subvention as partial payment for the services given. Isn't that what we call the "individual benefit" theory?

Mr. Butler:

As distinguished from benefit to a particular religion or religious group, yes.

Dr. Cary:

It really means that you cannot hold doggedly to an either/or position, but it means also that you have to scrutinize carefully the use to which any State aid is given. The whole thing comes down to the way in which aid is used. When it is used entirely to serve people, to help those who are handicapped, that is one thing. But if it is used to augment the institution, or in any way to promote the growth of the institution, that is an entirely different conception of "use."

Mr. Butler:

Except that the more the institution is built up, the more it is able to serve the community. We have certain services that are in

short supply—services to children, to the aged, and to the sick.
There are serious shortages here. Anyone knows this who has been
in need of hospitalization, or tried to get someone else into a hospital, and especially if he has tried to get an old person into a Home
for the Aged—if you can do that, you are a magician these days.

Dr. Cary: Always the emphasis is on the person—service to people.

The Chairman:

I see that. That is a very important point. Let us push it a little
bit farther. Take a home for children, for example. A part of the
care of children is, of course, their education. More and more we
are saying that education without a moral foundation is inadequate
And latterly we are saying that moral education includes some ele
ments of religious education—at the least, information about the
resources of religion for living. We have heard a great deal about
that from this platform.

Where are you going to draw the line? Here is a Protestant foster
home, and the education provided is bound to have definite religious
features; the same is true of a Catholic home or a Jewish home. How
are you going to make sure that public funds are not being used for
fostering a faith and therefore building up a particular religious
group—which the Federal Constitution, as interpreted by the Supreme Court, forbids?

Dr. Cary:

You are always going to have tension at that very point, and you
are going to have to work it out very carefully. But I maintain that
in actual practice, in the actual doing of the job, you learn the meaning of these tensions, you get more light upon them. In the actual
use of State aid, you gain insights that are helpful in the making
of policy respecting government grants and setting government
goals.

The Chairman:

Then you are saying, are you not, that you do not have a rule of
thumb to go by; but you have a broad principle, and you operate
in a spirit of service and with a will to maintain comity with all the
other elements of the community, and to solve problems as they
arise?

Dr. Cary: Yes.

Mr. Morrison:

Dr. Cary, there are two points in this connection that are covered by New York State law. I looked up the State welfare laws prior to this meeting, since I knew the matter would come up. One law provides—I believe it was passed in 1930—that the religious faith of children coming under the jurisdiction of public welfare officials shall be preserved and protected. The other, passed in 1924, provides that whenever a child is committed to an agency or institution under private auspices, such commitment shall as far as possible be made to an authorized agency under the control of persons of the same religious faith as the child. That seems to imply that the board of directors of that particular agency, or possibly the administration, shall be of the same faith.

Mr. Butler:

I think we ought to pause a minute here to say that all these agencies are incorporated under the Membership Corporation Law or by special act, either of the Legislature of the State or of the Congress. The agency is not a *church*. In New York State we have the Religious Corporations Law. All churches are incorporated under it. Under the Membership Corporations Law, we have hospitals, orphanages—a word we are not supposed to use any more under proper social-work terminology—we have hospitals, orphanages, old people's homes. All these are incorporated.

Incorporation has been necessitated by a rule of law that an unincorporated association is unable to take and hold property, particularly by devise or bequest. In order to get around that ancient rule—and it is an ancient rule and has no place in our present-day life—in order to get around that, these agencies are all incorporated. They are corporations, and they are referred to in that law as "agencies." That includes all, whether they are incorporated or unincorporated, but I do not know of any such agencies that are not incorporated.

The purpose back of that is disclosed in what is known as the "Religious Protection Clause." It is also in the Constitution of the State of New York. The purpose is to insure that no person shall be sent by a legal action to an institution of a religious faith other than his own—that is, under auspices of a religious group other than that to which he is related.

No public money is going for religious education in the ordinary sense because we have a much more stringent provision in the Constitution of the State of New York than in the Federal Constitution, forbidding the teaching of religion in a public school building. It goes far beyond the First Amendment in its specific restriction in so far as aid, direct or indirect, to any religious faith is concerned. And then they tacked onto it: "or a school in which a denominational tenet is taught." That is to say, whether such an institution is public or private, you cannot use tax money for its benefit. In so far as we are concerned here, we have no problem. The constitutional provision is explicit.

The Chairman:

You will remember that in the Zorach case, in which the United States Supreme Court upheld the New York plan of "released time" for religious education, the Court nevertheless declared that the public schools cannot engage in religious instruction.

Mr. Butler:

However we may dislike that restriction—and I think it is unsound—it is unquestionably in the Constitution of the State of New York, as it is in several United States Supreme Court decisions. But we are now on the third question you were going to ask.

Dr. Cary:

May I bring up just one thing more while we are on this subject? The essential thing is that a child should have a fair chance. And the important thing for all of us, whether we are in religious social work professionally or as volunteers, or in whatever capacity, is to work with the government to the end that the children are given a chance. If we work with government, we are in a far better position to influence policy on behalf of children.

The Chairman:

Mr. Butler is quite right: the third question that we agreed we would take up concerns the reconciliation of existing practice with the separation of church and state, which is established by the First

Amendment to the Federal Constitution, and which was made applicable to the States under the Fourteenth Amendment, when the Supreme Court so interpreted that Amendment. Are we on thin ice, in the light of a strict construction of the Constitution? Mr. Butler, you are a lawyer, will you speak to that first?

Mr. Butler:

It so happens that in 1899 that precise question was decided by the Supreme Court of the United States, in a case that involved Providence Hospital in the District of Columbia, which was a membership corporation, organized by special act of Congress. That is the old method and a very common method of incorporation. In 1899, the District of Columbia Commissioners—equivalent to a mayor—made a contract with the hospital whereby, on the appropriation of $30,000 by Congress, the hospital would erect two isolation buildings for contagious disease cases, and under the contract it would permanently dedicate two-thirds of its capacity to serving the poor sent to it by the Commissioners of the District of Columbia. In turn, the Commissioners would pay the hospital $250 a year for each patient sent there.

The contract was challenged in the case of *Bradfield vs. Roberts,* 175 U.S. 29, and the objection was made that tax money was being used to support a religious institution, and that this was a violation of the First Amendment because it tended toward an establishment of religion.

Of course, I do not think that when that Amendment was drafted the Founding Fathers had in mind many of the things that are being read into it at the present time. I think everyone will agree that the framers of the Constitution of the United States and the writers of the Declaration of Independence, and the people who settled the United States were God-fearing people.

But we are faced with an actual situation at the present time. I am reminded of the very brief remark which the Presiding Justice of the Appellate Division in this Department [of the State Supreme Court] once made to a young lawyer who was trying to persuade him that the Court's previous decisions were wrong. He said, "Maybe we're wrong, but we're sot in it." And maybe they are wrong in their interpretation of the First Amendment, but it is clear that whether the Supreme Court of the United States has recognized the existence of the "wall of separation" or has actually *created* the wall, we have it, so one cannot use tax money for purposes of religious education. There is no question about that.

The same contention was urged in this District of Columbia case to which I have referred. But the Court said in effect: "This hospital is a creature of the state. It is not a religion, nor is it religious. It is under the auspices of a religious organization." And the Court held that the contract was not invalidated by the fact that a particular church—and here unquestionably a religious order, the Sisters of Charity of Emmitsburg, Maryland, a Roman Catholic Order—had established the hospital and maintained it. The Court said that even the fact of control by a religious body would not invalidate the contract as a violation of the separation of church and state. This was because no aid was being given to a religion. The aid is being given to a civil entity created by the state. And so the Court held that the appropriation in that instance was valid. That case has been cited in most such discussions as this, since it is one of the earlier cases in which this principle was laid down.

The Chairman:

What would you say to the application of that principle, Mr Morrison? How far would that interpretation take us?

Mr. Morrison:

I would say that Mr. Butler's interpretation is altogether valid. My personal feeling in this matter always has been this: the church— the religious social work agency—has always had a pioneer role. Religious agencies were the pioneers, as Dr. Cary pointed out, in the nursery school field; they were the pioneers in developing the case-work method, and in the use of psychiatry.

There has always been extremely close scrutiny of public funds used for anything except primarily custodial care—in other words, the administration of actual relief. There has been a great deal of discussion in community councils and community chests concerning the allocation of public funds to a private social agency under religious auspices to cover operating expense—in other words, to cover a *pro rata* share of administrative expense, psychiatric social-work expense, etc. That has given rise to some debate, I know, in the legislature as to whether public funds should be used for that expensive type of work in order to help individuals to help themselves.

I feel that religious social work, in and of itself, has been a torch-bearer in the entire field. There is no doubt about it. Historically, this has been borne out time and time again. I consider it a privilege that we as citizens of this great country enjoy, that our tax money is being used to help religious social agencies promote the great work that they are doing to help people.

When it comes to religious education, I fear with Mr. Butler that there is something here requiring much scrutiny and careful evaluation.

The Chairman: Suppose you apply the principle that every corporation is a civil entity—am I quoting you correctly, Mr. Butler?

Mr. Butler: Yes.

The Chairman:

I think you made the distinction clear: if a corporation has a religious character—that is, if it is incorporated as a religious body—that is one thing. If it is not so incorporated, it is something else; even though it is under religious auspices, it is a civil entity. That is the principle, and it is important. I think it has very seldom been pointed out in such discussions as this.

Mr. Butler:

I think the confusion arises because not all the States have made this sharp distinction between religious and civil corporations. A religious corporation's task is entirely concerned with religion.

Take, for example, the Roman Catholic Church. The law in New York specifies that every church is a religious corporation; in the Catholic Church the president of the corporation is the bishop of the diocese; the vice-president is the vicar general; the treasurer is the pastor of the parish, and there are two other trustees—lay trustees. These constitute the governing body. Outside the field of religion as sharply defined, one gets into such questions as who owns the property and who is the boss. These matters are confirmed by law, and you might be surprised to know that where they are not clearly set forth there are many serious law suits as to who owns the property and who has the "say." In the event of the death of somebody, what becomes of the property? A lot of purely mundane questions come up in the life of a membership corporation under religious auspices.

The Chairman:

Suppose a school is incorporated as an educational institution and is "civil" in that sense, but is a parochial school or some other kind of religious school, Jewish, Catholic, or Protestant, then what is to prevent that school, which has a definitely religious purpose, from receiving public funds under the judicial rule we have been discussing?

Mr. Butler:

The Constitution of this State denies any public money for educational purposes to any school, incorporated or unincorporated, in which a denominational tenet is taught.

The Chairman:

But suppose we waive that for the moment. Suppose we are not in New York. Considering the Federal Constitution alone, would you say that the Supreme Court decisions to which we have referred would prevent a school under religious auspices from receiving any public funds?

Mr. Butler:

It is not safe to prophesy what the Supreme Court is going to say in a particular case, but I do not think that it is so much a matter of the religious auspices as of the religious tenets taught in the school. I am convinced that, unless it completely reverses itself, the Supreme Court of the United States would hold that anything done in a public school which is directly related to the teaching of religion is a violation of the First Amendment.

Mr. Morrison:

I have reviewed the Social Legislation Digest for the past few years, and I think Mr. Butler is right. All sorts of legislation have been on the books these past few years in regard to assistance to private organizations which might be under the auspices of a specific religious group. They always specify what that assistance is, and what it will be used for—civilian defense, disaster relief, training of doctors and nurses, and so on. In other words, the laws are very specific.

The Chairman:

It seems to emerge from what has been said that the State recognizes that it has an equity, so to say, in the preservation of religious rights. A child becomes a ward of the State, or an old person becomes a resident of a tax-supported Home for the Aged. The community has a stake in taking care of these people, and the community also has a concern that their religious needs shall be met. So that means that this "wall of separation" is perhaps something less than absolute.

Mr. Butler:

May I make a remark on that very point? When a man is convicted of a serious crime and sentenced to prison for life, the Constitutions of the State of New York and of the United States guarantee to him freedom of worship according to the dictates of his conscience. They are not going to let him pick a church that he may go out to on Sunday, but they bring the church to him, and the erection of a church at Dannemora Prison has been sustained as not in violation of the separation of church and state.

Over the years there has been a tendency to build the "wall of separation" higher than was originally intended. We should respect the government. Duly constituted authority decides what we can and cannot do. But the government was never intended to deprive citizens of freedom to obey the Commandment, "Thou shalt love thy neighbor," and whether or not you believe that to be a Divine Commandment, religion is one of the motivating forces that constrain the individual to help his neighbor, and the state should not step in and say that tax funds can be used only if they are disbursed by a tax-paid individual.

The Chairman: Did you want to speak to that, Dr. Cary?

Dr. Cary:

This is not exactly on that point, but there is one great danger that I fear. In this whole matter of public assistance, if instead of cooperating with the officials we start quarreling about it, we play into the hands of those who are for "economy at any price." It is easy to get involved in politics with the result that we shall be left without the funds we all need.

The Chairman:

During the Depression, under the administration of W.P.A., I think funds were made available for parish work to a considerable extent—that is, for recreation and education. Did that create a problem? I never heard much controversy over it.

Mr. Butler:

W.P.A. did not actually put teachers in a parochial school. They might have sent in some people who were on relief to do some kind of work.

Dr. Cary:

There was some criticism at times. Help was given to redecorate churches or new school buildings.

The Chairman: You would all agree that would be an abuse?

Mr. Morrison: A misuse of public funds.

The Chairman:

If I understand you, gentlemen, you are really saying that the basis for any kind of state aid to the kinds of work we have been discussing is the fact that the state takes account of the need of the individual or the family concerned—not the claims of an institution or agency. It seems to be emerging from this discussion that the community recognizes basic needs of individuals, especially perhaps, of children and of the aged, and that the state has a right and a duty to assist agencies that operate under religious auspices in meeting these needs, but that direct benefits to a religious body or agency are excluded.

Have you in the audience questions you want to ask the panel?

Question: Under the principle that you gave in summary, would it not be possible for the government agency to build parochial schools, on the theory that it is an aid to the person, just as it might be possible to give lunches?

The Chairman: Where do we draw the line?

Mr. Morrison: They would draw the line at a capital building funds expenditure.

Mr. Butler: The only time money has been given for such capital expenditure in New York State is under a recently passed law which grants money for the erection of hospitals. There you come into the area of health and welfare services. We have a provision in the Constitution of the State of New York, and in the Education Law, the Social Welfare Law, and the Public Health Law that wherever a public agency gives health or welfare services to public school children, the same service must be given to all children without regard to the school they attend. It is to the benefit of the community that the children in a parochial or other non-public school be examined to see whether they are healthy, whether they need glasses, whether they need hearing aids, whether they are in need of immediate physical assistance. That is not a service to the school. That is a service to the child. We have a definite principle laid down in the decisions of the United States Supreme Court which distinguishes between service to the child and aid given directly to a religious institution or agency. The latter is barred.

Question: I should like to press this question in relation to the hospitals. I see the possibility of government funds being used for hospitals where evangelism of one kind or another can very easily be carried on and may even be a major concern.

Mr. Butler:

I would say that whatever evangelism occurs in a hospital is *per accidens* [incidental, and apart from purpose and design]. That will occur anywhere. For instance, there are teachers who will try to teach some particular doctrine in a public school. Of course, if they are caught, they will be stopped. In a hospital, the staff members are so busy that they have to rely upon large numbers of volunteers. There is another accidental sectarian benefit in the conduct of a hospital run by a religious group. One feels more kindly disposed to a religious group if he has had a wholesome experience in its hospital. But that is an accidental thing that cannot be controlled.

The Chairman (concluding the discussion):

I have been wishing that the Supreme Court could develop that *per accidens* principle. Take, for instance, the chaplaincy supported by public funds. I do not believe that any of our courts would invalidate the chaplaincy on the basis of the First Amendment. Here the incidental benefit to the religious body concerned is obvious and substantial. It is perfectly clear that the Methodist chaplains, for example, in their services render valuable aid to the Methodist Church. But this is incidental, and it seems to me that the courts would render an important public service by clarifying the distinction between direct and intentional "aid to religion" which is barred, and the incidental increment of benefit to a religious group or agency that results inevitably from wholly legitimate public grants. What I am suggesting is that a distinction which is already implicit in court decisions might well be made explicit. But, of course, I am not a lawyer!

XII

REFLECTION AND PERSPECTIVE

BY

F. ERNEST JOHNSON

The purpose of this final paper in our series is to bring what has gone before into perspective, and to point up what seem to me to be significant insights and emergent issues. In doing so I shall inevitably express my own special concerns. This is going to be, of course, a selective review. I wish to stress particular contributions that have been made to our thinking and certain issues that seem to me to call for emphasis.

The church's primary concern, Professor Swift reminded us, is not with social welfare; it is not with any program of activities. And when I use the word "church" you will understand that I use it generically, to denote a particular religious community. The church's primary concern is with the vertical dimension of life. As Professor Tillich said when discussing religious symbolism in our series in 1952, "Religion is concerned with the ultimate." Organized religion has a responsibility for keeping men aware of the ultimate concerns, the ultimate requirements of life. So it may properly be said that all manner of social expression of religious motive, all of the horizontal out-reach of religious initiative and effort, is secondary, from a religious viewpoint, to the vertical dimension of experience which gives the imperative to act. I think it was appropriate that we should be reminded of this fact at the outset.

But Professor Swift also took pains to point out that in its major preoccupation with ultimate spiritual realities religion must never lose sight of the human situation. Moreover, it must entertain a hopeful view of human potentialities. This cuts across a contemporary emphasis in Protestant theology which tends to devaluate man, to make all human initiative relatively unimportant and to make the divine initiative all in all. This, as many of you will recognize, is a revival of an extreme Calvinistic emphasis in theology. Professor Swift, I take it, is a liberal in that respect: he sees reality in the appeal of the "social gospel." It is important to be realistic about the evil propensities that human beings manifest; but unless we envisage the possible progressive improvement of the human situation, it is idle to talk of the relation of religion to social welfare.

I find it necessary on many occasions to stress the fact that the ethical realism in contemporary Protestant theology does no necessary violence to the social gospel; for the heart of the social gospel—which has Catholic and Jewish equivalents expressed in different terminology—was always the requirement that the ethics implicit in Christianity be made applicable to the structure of human relationships, as well as to individual lives. That demands ethical realism of the first order. And a secular concomitant of this, of course, is the continual growth of that social concern whose political symbol has come to be the welfare state. Professor Swift evidently believes, as I believe, that the pattern of the democratic welfare state has come to stay.

Social work under Protestant auspices seems to be expanding. That certainly is the impression one gains from Canon Pepper's paper, and it raises a question in my mind whether the Protestant pattern of social work may be gradually changing. Mr. Davies in his paper quoted something that I had written a number of years ago concerning the nature of Protestant social work and noting the emphasis in American Protestantism on social effort through non-sectarian agencies rather than the building of distinctively Protestant agencies and institutions. There are exceptions, of course, but broadly speaking, especially in the field of case-work, that has been the Protestant pattern.

However, I think it is a fair inference from what has been said here that the Protestant churches are becoming more institution-minded in this area and are tending to put more stress upon distinctively Protestant institutions and agencies. I venture to say that if this is true it marks a change whose significance should be carefully pondered. It marks a tendency to turn toward the Jewish and the Catholic patterns, which make large place for institutional enterprise controlled and supported by, and informed with, a religious faith, and related to a religious community. This tendency is proper, I think, for a religious minority which has its own cultural norms to maintain against the pressures of a social environment that is largely alien to it. For a majority group, however, such as American Protestantism comprises, the maintenance of a distinctive set of agencies and institutions is less easy to justify. We shall return to this subject later.

In any event, all religious work that is aimed at the spiritual enrichment of a parish or a community has social welfare aspects, which should, as Canon Pepper urged, be integrated with the entire program of the church. Social work, as he sees it, is not simply something that is done for others, but a normal part of the program of the church, envisaged in its message and encompassed in its worship. I think that in this series all the expositions of religious social work in actual practice reflect this philosophy.

That statement, "Social work is not something done for others, but a normal part of the service of the church," is reminiscent of a difference of opinion that developed many years ago between Mary E. Richmond and Edward T. Devine, both of whom I knew very well and greatly admired. Mr. Devine, an eminent authority in his field, was disposed to look at social work always through the eyes of the professional worker. He saw it as something done in the name of a community and with community resources, by specially trained persons, for the less fortunate. But Mary Richmond, herself a master of social-work technique, said in effect, "I don't at all like the idea that social work is something done for some people by others. Social work should be an aspect of human relations in a wholesome community." I remember her saying, at a time when there was a great deal of relief work to be done: "Don't let people get the idea that social work is just a professional enterprise. Everybody who has a job in the backyard to give to somebody who needs a job is in the position to do social work."

Monsignor O'Grady, in his discussion of Catholic social work, contributed significantly to this line of thought. He is very much concerned that social work shall not be excessively institutionalized, that it shall not fall into the hands of, or under the control of, a coterie. He keeps the whole community in mind and is greatly concerned that social work be carried on in a democratic fashion. Like Miss Richmond, he puts much stress on voluntary lay participation. Although the Roman Church has a hierarchical structure, Catholic leaders are sometimes able to see the implications of democratic theory for political, social, and economic life more clearly than many of us do.

The Catholic Church in the Old World, and in "Catholic countries" generally, is an example of what has been called the "church type" of organization, as opposed to the "sect type" represented by most of our Protestant bodies, at least in the early stages of their development. That is to say, the Roman Church normally conceives itself as coextensive with the community. The same tends to be true of Protestantism and Eastern Orthodoxy in countries where these faiths prevail. In Europe, until recently, it was a commonplace that one's religion was bound up with his nationality. The faith went with the flag. A visitor in Europe before World War II was likely to be impressed by the fact that a Pole took his allegiance to the Roman Church as a matter of course, and a Greek took his Orthodoxy in the same way. Where the people are religiously homogeneous the church tends to be "the community on its knees."

Over against that pattern is the sectarian type of religious organization whose creed, ritual, and discipline tend to set it off from the community as a whole. Most of our Protestant churches in America can be traced to sectarian movements. Our largest single Protestant body, the Methodist (to which I happen to belong) was distinctly a sectarian movement at the start, an offshoot of the Anglican Church. But the Methodist Church has now grown to such great proportions that it is virtually a cross-section of the community as a whole. It has in its fellowship "some of everybody," sociologically and culturally speaking. Moreover, and most significantly, the major Protestant bodies are sufficiently alike that together they constitute a religious majority—that is, in the nation as a whole—which has given to this country a sort of Protestant ethos. That, I am persuaded, is the main reason why Protestants in this country have so readily accepted secular forms of education and social work.

The Roman Catholic Church in America, in contrast to its Old World pattern, has been impelled by its minority role to react protectively against the prevailing culture, as spiritually alien. The Catholic Church represents, in large measure, a culture of its own and it seeks to maintain a program of education and social services within the Catholic community and expressive of its own life and purposes. To some non-Catholics this seems a threat to cultural unity in America. It may also be viewed as an expression of cultural pluralism, which many regard as an American cultural ideal.

Although the subject is painful, I am constrained to call attention to the recent controversy in the Health and Welfare Council of New York over planned parenthood, which illustrates the tensions that sectarian differences, rooted in deep convictions, can create within organized social work. Many non-Catholics were aggrieved and annoyed over Catholic unwillingness to remain in the Welfare and Health Council if an agency whose purpose was to promote planned parenthood was allowed to remain in it; but the fact remains that a tenet of faith so very strong as the one here involved could not fail to register in Catholic social policy. To the Catholic Church birth control is as unacceptable as Communism. I wish more careful thought and more consultation could have been given to that issue because involved in it is the whole question of the relation of an organized religious body—a faith group—to the community as a whole.

Jewish social work shows a degree of integration, it seems to me, with the life of the Jewish community that is not realized by other faith groups. None of us can fail to be impressed with the significance of *community* in Jewish history and teaching—in particular, with the continuing idea of a "covenant" which is rooted in the Old Testament and which gives a peculiar character to the Jewish people. And somehow Judaism—and I think this is true of its three branches, though perhaps not equally so—has been able to maintain a continuity of thought and practice between what is distinctively religious and what is social and ethical. Professor Swift gave us a quotation from Rabbi David de Sola Pool which is worth recalling here:

In Judaism religion was never allowed to be divorced from the regulations of the sociolegal code and become limited to an emotion, or a quest of personal salvation, or a practice of ecclesiastical ceremony. The establishment of just relations between capital and labor, master and servant, between citizen and alien, between rich and poor, so repeatedly and explicitly called for in the Mosaic, prophetic, and rabbinic code is just as much an essential of the religion of Judaism as are the spiritual experiences with which religion is popularly identified.[1]

I became impressed many years ago with that quality of Judaism which makes religion a total ritual of living. The comprehensive paper presented by Dr. Landesman made this clear. It gave us an insight into the peculiar genius of Jewish social work as an expression of the Jewish faith and of the integrity of the Jewish community. You remember Dr. Landesman's reference to *"zedakah,"* [2] the principle of righteousness, of justice, which is implicit in all Jewish teaching. Reference is often made to the great "medieval synthesis" of thought and life as an outstanding achievement of Christendom. It seems to me that the historic Jewish synthesis of law, wisdom, and ritual of worshipful living is a proportionately comparable achievement.

Before going further with this review I must refer again to Protestant social work in the light of what we have noted in the Catholic and Jewish patterns. If the latter can justify their cultural separateness, why, one may ask, should not Protestantism have its own comparable setup? The logical answer, it seems to me, is given in what has already been said about the influence of the Protestant ethos

[1] See footnote 1, p. 4.
[2] See pp. 51 ff.

upon American culture. The considerations that have impelled Catholics and Jews to develop and maintain at great expense their own institutional services and programs are not applicable to the majority religious group. Non-sectarian social work in this country is bound to reflect in considerable degree the religious ethos that prevails in our culture and has profoundly influenced our history. It is hardly too much to say that a heavy burden of proof rests upon Protestant enterprise when it turns in the direction of paralleling social-welfare activities conducted under non-sectarian auspices.

It should go without saying that Protestants have a collective obligation to see that ample provision is made for contact and prompt referral in the case of every person and family of Protestant background that may need some social service. This is an important function of a Protestant welfare agency.

It should be noted that the insightful paper by Mr. Bigham sets forth a basis for collaboration between ministers and social workers that is entirely consistent with a policy of full collaboration with non-sectarian agencies. He has made, I think, a distinctive and illuminating contribution to the literature of this subject.

The spiritual phase of social work which Mr. Mayo discussed is implicit in the worker-client relationship. It is a matter of interpersonal relations. Wherever you have personalities coming into encounter, wherever you have a personality becoming the vehicle for the communication of worthful experience, there is a spiritual force at work. And Mr. Mayo gave us the triangulation—the individual, the group, and the community; case-work, group work, and community relations on a broad scale.

The spiritual factor is not something that can be isolated; it is in the very structure of the relations between human beings. It is not something that is injected into social work by virtue of its being conducted under religious auspices. It is present wherever excellence is achieved in social work, regardless of the auspices. The significant thing so far as church or synagogue is concerned, is that the person who carries on social work in the name of and representing a religious organization, or agency, or parish, is representing a corporate religious resource which he makes available to the client. That worker is in some sense a symbol of resources in the background, the resources of the religious community which it offers for the rehabilitation of a broken body or spirit, or to anyone who is struggling to achieve a more abundant life.]

The emphasis placed on the influence of environment is timely. It is a grievous error, too often made these days, to deprecate a concern over social environment as a determinative force. Environment cannot assure salvation, but it can come close to insuring damnation. The Protestant concern for a social gospel, the Jewish preoccupation with social justice, the Catholic zeal for social action—these are all oriented toward the remaking of environment. We need no further demonstration that the potentialities of the human spirit are permitted to unfold and develop or are restrained, restricted, or destroyed, depending in great measure on the character of the social environment. And let us never forget the function of religion as a factor in determining that environment.

Repeatedly in this series attention has been directed toward special preparation for social work on the part of ministers. I will venture a *caveat,* however, concerning this matter of ministerial specialization. I am thrilled over the development of new professional skills on the part of the ministry. The clinical training of ministers so that they become personal workers with psychiatric understanding and insight, the placing of ministers with both theological and clinical training in hospitals and correctional institutions—all this is matter for rejoicing. But there is more than a little danger that such a specialist may become more of a psychologist, or a psychiatrist, or a health expert, or a neighborhood organizer than he is a minister.]

For years, when we in the Federal Council of Churches were exploring the field of the relation between religion and health, we looked for a minister who would add to his equipment the wisdom and the techniques of the psychiatrist, but who would not cease to be primarily a minister. We eventually succeeded, but it took a long time. Too often when we found someone who was greatly enamored of psychiatry, he was in danger of becoming a pseudo-psychiatrist while his ministerial equipment fell into disuse. The minister and the parish worker need all the knowledge of social work, including psychiatric social work, that they can acquire, but their place in the community depends ultimately on their ability to do what no one else can do.

The social worker, in every area of activity and by the very nature of his profession, has to pay the price of society's educational neglect. He must deal with people as they have come to be, resisting the temptation to conclude that human beings are by nature "like that."

The care of children and the care of the aged, discussed for us by Miss Lenroot and Miss Wahlstrom, have an important place in a book on religious social work. Let me say with emphasis that with respect to what I have called the Protestant pattern—which prevailingly finds outlet for energies and resources through non-sectarian channels—the care of children and the care of the aged are exceptions. When it is necessary to establish foster homes for young children, we have to integrate care with religious education, and this can be done best in a definitely religious environment. At the other end of the age scale, when people reach the point where they have to be cared for in congregate homes, their domicile inevitably tends more and more to become their church, as well. Child care and care of the aged, complementing each other in the life cycle, place upon church and synagogue very special responsibilities for creating homes that are centers of spiritual nurture. Not all aged people, to be sure, who seek collective domicile will prefer a home under definitely religious auspices. Indeed, some may feel that they can bear separation from their denominational kind! But I think many of the people in our church homes would be very unhappy indeed if they could not maintain their consciousness of membership in their own particular religious community during their old age.

When we came to a discussion of the legal basis of public aid for social work, I think we arrived at a significant conclusion in that informing discussion participated in by Mr. Butler, Dr. Cary and Mr. Morrison. I tried to formulate it at the conclusion of the period and need not repeat it here.[3] Suffice it to say that where basic needs of persons are concerned, the nice categories of law and jurisprudence tend to break down. It is in such discussions as we had here about

[3] See p. 169.

the rulings of courts and the needs of human beings that one gets the full force of the late Justice Holmes's great dictum: "The life of the law has not been logic; it has been experience."

I am now going to do something that may seem rash. Knowing the hazards of prediction and disclaiming any prophetic adequacy or intention I shall nevertheless venture to set down what seem to me some probable developments in the years ahead—that is, sufficiently probable to warrant our taking account of them in formulating future strategy.

First, the expansion of public initiative and effort in social work is likely to continue as the range of community responsibility increases. I think we may take it for granted that while there will be periods of recession, public welfare work is going to play an increasing role in the long run. This seems to be a natural result of social and political forces that are now at work. As the social conscience is sharpened, as the range of the social responsibility felt by the citizen increases, more and more kinds of social work are likely to come under the community umbrella. This does not mean that the government is going to monopolize welfare. Perhaps I should say there are two community umbrellas, one private and the other public. But the sheer magnitude of the task of lifting the general level of health and well-being seems bound to make private efforts inadequate. I think we have to take that for granted.

Second, there is likely to be, concomitantly, a limitation of private resources—not uniformly, for there will be ups and downs, but continuing indefinitely—available for private welfare work, whether secular or religious. It seems improbable that in the foreseeable future government will cease absorbing a vast amount of the social surplus.

Third, as a result of this situation non-sectarian agencies are likely to have to restrict their efforts, perhaps progressively, to 1. intensive social work on behalf of individuals and families in situations that make planned, sustained, and cooperative social work possible—individuals and families who are able and willing to learn to help themselves; and 2. experimental, exploratory work in which the community as a whole is not ready to engage. I may illustrate that latter point by reference to the function of private schools.

Educators are, in general, committed to the public-school system as a dominant educational pattern, but they nevertheless are wont to welcome private schools to the extent that they are ready to engage in research, experimentation, and demonstration, to open up new curricular areas, and to devise new methods. All public enterprise needs the guiding and corrective influence of private undertakings that have greater freedom. Non-sectarian social agencies—and I wish, with Mr. Davies, that we could dispense with that negative term, "non-sectarian"—are the natural instrumentality for such exploration in the social-work field. It should be noted here that the amazing vista now opening before us as a result of automation in industry may yield its most significant result in the creation of leisure on a grand scale that will usher in a new era in volunteer social and educational work.

Fourth, I see the church and the synagogue under similar pressure in the years ahead to concentrate on distinctive tasks. Are they not likely—missionary enterprise aside—to confine themselves increasingly to work that is definitely related to one religious community? Locally, this means a parish or its equivalent. No one can be sure about this, but I think that is the indicated trend. This means more efforts to serve a continuing "clientele," a continuing membership, and less of widely varied "services," such as we have seen under the banner of the institutional church where the church goes into a community and tries to do a little something for everybody. I think that pattern is outmoded. More and more, it now appears, our churches will have to limit themselves to sustained efforts to enrich the lives of a continuing membership, a parish community. Within that area of responsibility there is nothing, of course, that a church may not properly do in the way of social effort if it is clearly indicated at a given time and in the particular situation. Mr. Spike gave us an impressive illustration of what consecrated inventive genius can do in a local parish.

This does not mean a *narrower* ministry, for parish work at its best has an unlimited horizontal thrust, but it does mean a more *intensive* ministry. Out of the religious community—Protestant, Catholic, Jewish—should come inspired leaders and intelligently directed resources for both public and private social work, that is, under both public and private secular auspices. In other words, the relationship of the church to social work may be more and more of the sort envisaged by Mr. Davies in his discriminating analysis: the community, under the inspiration of religiously nurtured persons, seeing the potency of religious motivation and the necessity for religious institutions, will want the people into whose hands professional work is entrusted to be the kind of people who are reared in a religious fellowship. If I am right, the main contribution to social work that is to be looked for from church and synagogue will be in terms of services rendered by persons whose vision has been clarified and motives cultivated through the ministries of religion and who will devote themselves, some in a professional and some in a lay capacity, to promoting the general welfare.

INDEX